THE EARTH ROLLS ON

BY BILLY JOE SHAVER

Honky Tonk Hero

by Billy Joe Shaver

ASSISTED BY BRAD REAGAN

Honky Tonk Hero

UNIVERSITY OF TEXAS PRESS, AUSTIN

Publication of this book
was aided by the generous support of
Brad Moore.

Requests for permission to reproduce material from this work
should be sent to Permissions, University of Texas Press,
P.O. Box 7819, Austin, TX 78713-7819.
utpress.utexas.edu/rp-form

♾ The paper used in this book meets the minimum requirements
of ANSI/NISO Z39.48-1992 (R1997) (Permanence of Paper).

LIBRARY OF CONGRESS CATALOGING-IN-PUBLICATION DATA
Shaver, Billy Joe.
Honky tonk hero / by Billy Joe Shaver ; assisted by Brad Reagan. —1st ed.
p. cm.
Includes complete lyrics to the recorded songs written by Billy Joe Shaver.

1. Shaver, Billy Joe. 2. Country musicians—United States—Biography. I. Reagan,
Brad. II. Shaver, Billy Joe. Songs. Texts. III. Title.
ML420.S534A3 2005
782.421642'092—dc22

2004019569

ISBN 978-1-4773-2396-0, paperback

contents

□

□

I WAS NOT EVEN BORN YET when my father first tried to kill me.

It was June and the evening light had started to fade, but it was still hotter than nine kinds of hell. We were outside of Corsicana, a little cotton town in northeast Texas, and I was in my mother's belly, two months from entering the world.

Buddy Shaver was convinced that my mother, Victory, was cheating on him. That was bullshit, and he probably knew it. But he'd been drinking. My father was half-French, half-Blackfoot Sioux, and one-hundred-percent mean. He drank a lot, and the booze didn't mix well with his Indian blood. You know there are some guys who are just born naturally strong, with big shoulders and a chiseled upper body even though they never work a lick at it? That was my father, and my mother didn't have a chance.

It's just a story I've heard, told by family members who don't enjoy the re-telling. But I can see it as clearly as if I was there. They were standing next to a small stock tank with black, still water. It was the middle of nowhere, with no roads or houses in sight. Who knows what he told her to get her out there, or whether she knew what was coming when they stopped there? He held nothing back, yet his cold gray eyes showed no emotion as he beat her within an inch of her life. When she was down, he stomped her with his cowboy boots until she stopped struggling. Then he tossed her limp body into the water like a sack of potatoes. Years later, when I was a grown man, my momma couldn't stand to be around me when I wore cowboy boots—she never could forget what they did to her that night.

Momma laid there for hours until an old Mexican man showed up to water his cattle. Even though he knew my kinfolk pretty well, he didn't recognize her at first. He thought she was dead. But she spoke to him through the bruises and the blood, and he threw her over the back of his horse and carried her home.

The violence of that night set the stage for my childhood: It's the reason father left, it's the reason my mother didn't want me, and it's the reason I went to live with my loving grandmother. In many ways, I think that night is the reason I write country songs.

When you get right down to it, country music is essentially the blues, and that night introduced me to the blues. In the years since then, they've never left me. I've lost parts of three fingers, broke my back, suffered a heart attack and a quadruple bypass, had a steel plate put in my neck and 136 stitches in my head, fought drugs and booze, spent the money I had, and buried my wife, son, and mother in the span of one year.

But I'm not here to complain or ask for pity. Life is hard for everybody, just in different ways. I'm not proud of my misfortune—I'm proud of my survival. For years, my family kept a bundle of life insurance on me because they were sure I would be the first to go. But as I write this, at sixty-four years of age, I'm still here and they are all gone.

The question is—why? That's something I've been thinking about a lot lately.

Throughout my career as a songwriter, I've just written songs about me—the good and the bad, the funny and the sad. I've written songs about other people, but I don't sing other people's songs. They're just little poems about my life, and I've never pretended they were anything more. Despite all my ups and downs, I've never been to therapy or rehab or any of that stuff. The songs are my therapy.

But after my shows, people always come up to me and thank me for writing those songs. They tell me about their lives, and how a song of mine helped them through a tough patch or made them smile during a difficult time. Sometimes they say I inspired them—that if I can make it through my life, they can damn sure get through theirs. When we're done talking, I give them a hug and tell them I love them. I know exactly where they are coming from.

My point is, it's truly a miracle I survived that night by that stock tank, and I don't mean that the way most people say it—like it's a lucky break. I think God allowed me to live. He wanted me to tell my story.

CLOCKWISE FROM TOP: *My father, Buddy, and my mother, Tincie. My father was French and Blackfoot. My Mother was Scots/Irish. ◆ Me and Patricia on our stepfather's parents' farm in Elk, Texas. I'm already starting to look like an outlaw. ◆ My grandmother and me. She raised me until I was twelve years old. She used to bounce me on her knee and tell me I would sing on the stage of the Grand Ole Opry. She was right. ◆ I joined the Navy the day I turned seventeen. Here I am with my mother. ◆ Me as a baby.*

CLOCKWISE FROM TOP LEFT: *A couple of my grade-school pictures.* ◆ *Willie the Wandering Gypsy and me. Since Willie and I were both from Central Texas and both a little bit crazy, we got along good from the start. The night my son Eddy died, we were scheduled to play a gig in Austin. Willie kindly filled in for Eddy on guitar.* ◆ *In Nashville, the Texans stuck together. That's Waylon Jennings on the far right. In 1972, Waylon decided to do an album of my songs. That's Coach Darrell Royal on the left, and me and a friend in the middle.* ◆ *My wife Brenda and I during better days.*

CLOCKWISE FROM TOP LEFT: *Eddy, my beautiful baby boy.* ◆ *Eddy rode horses before he could walk. He started playing the guitar when he was just a boy and was playing in my band by the time he was twelve.* ◆ *We weren't the most normal family but we had a good time when we were together.* ◆ *When Eddy and I put out* Tramp on Your Street *people said it was the second coming of Billy Joe Shaver.* ◆ *Eddy.*

CLOCKWISE FROM TOP LEFT: *In 2001, the Americana Music Association gave me its Lifetime Achievement Award for songwriting. It was the first award I'd ever received for my music.* ◆ *Me and my good friend Robert Duvall. He appeared in my video for "Freedom's Child." He also co-produced a documentary about my life that premiered in 2004.* ◆ *At the premier of the documentary, produced and directed by Luciana Pedraza.*

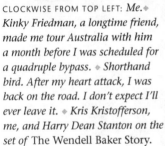

CLOCKWISE FROM TOP LEFT: *Me.* ◆ *Kinky Friedman, a longtime friend, made me tour Australia with him a month before I was scheduled for a quadruple bypass.* ◆ *Shorthand bird. After my heart attack, I was back on the road. I don't expect I'll ever leave it.* ◆ *Kris Kristofferson, me, and Harry Dean Stanton on the set of* The Wendell Baker Story.

CLOCKWISE FROM TOP: *Rosie Flores and me. She's a great writer, singer, guitar player, and friend.* ◆ *Me, Rosie, and Eddy. We were close friends. When Brenda died of cancer, it tore Eddy to pieces. They were like brother and sister. Eddy was thirty-eight when he died. He was my best friend.* ◆ *Me.*

Honky Tonk Hero

chapter one

Jesus Was Our Savior and Cotton Was Our King

□

The wagons was a-rollin' with a cobble-colored sound
When me and little David rode our first load into town
The cotton gin was a-ginnin' out the pennies for the pound
Like a giant vacuum cleaner sucking lint up off the ground

Our freckled faces sparkled then like diamonds in the rough
With smiles that smelled of snaggled teeth and good ol' Garrett snuff
If I could, I would be tradin' all this fatback for the lean
When Jesus was our Savior and cotton was our king

WE ARE COUNTRY PEOPLE, always have been. My family tree is full of field hands and farmers, people who lived off the land and worked with their hands.

My grandparents on my mother's side were originally from the Texarkana area but moved to Corsicana since it was known as a town that was friendly toward sharecroppers. Located about fifty-three miles northeast of Waco, Corsicana was a farming community and one of the top cotton-producing towns in Texas during the late nineteenth and early twentieth centuries. Several of the railroads came right through town, which made it easy to get the crops to market. Not just cotton, but corn, tobacco, and pecans too. But cotton was king. The gin there covered five city blocks downtown and was said to be the largest in the world for a time.

In 1894, the town really started to boom. That's when the town leaders paid these boys from Kansas to come down and find more water for the growing community, and they hit oil instead. The townsfolk were so pissed off that they didn't pay the drillers their fee. As it turned out, that was the first discovery of oil in Texas, and no one had a clue about how it was going to change the area, not to mention the entire state. Of course, several businesses started up in Corsicana to take advantage of the discovery. You've probably heard of two of them: Mobil and Texaco.

But, as I said, my family wasn't involved in oil. We worked the fields. We were poor but so was everybody around us. You either owned land—and we sure as hell didn't—or you sharecropped and got by one sack at a time.

My grandparents had seven kids and the youngest was a girl they named Victory, because she was born the day the First World War ended. That was my mother. I always loved that name—I used it as the title of one of my albums—but everyone called her Tincie instead, because she was so small. She grew into a beauty, with a petite figure, sky-blue eyes, and red hair that told of the fire inside her.

At eighteen, Tincie married Buddy Shaver, though her parents weren't too happy about it. Buddy, who never learned to read or write, was a bootlegger, moonshiner, and bare-knuckle fighter who was just about the meanest son-of-a-bitch in the county. My mother was tough, though, and I guess she thought she could tame him. I don't know for sure why she married that man—even decades later, she wouldn't talk about it.

Buddy and Tincie had a daughter, Patricia, who was two years old when Buddy erupted out by that stock tank. Tincie recovered from the beating, but just barely. That ended the marriage, of course, and Tincie also made it clear that she wasn't going to raise Buddy Shaver's son.

"If it comes out a boy," she said. "I'm gone."

I was born August 16, 1939. Tincie wasn't quite true to her word—she stayed about a month and then took the first chance that came her way.

It was September, so the cotton crop was ready for picking. That meant she was needed in the fields whether or not she had two young children. So there she was, picking cotton in the midday sun—me on her back, Patricia riding on the cotton sack behind her, and a halo of gnats and flies swirling around her head.

Then Blanche Williams came rolling up in her black Cadillac.

Blanche was the proud owner of the Green Gables honky tonk outside of Waco, about an hour southwest of Corsicana. Every few weeks, she'd drive around the country in search of good-looking, small-town girls who could read, write, and charm customers out of their cash. On this day, Blanche settled on Tincie, her red hair glowing amid the sea of black and white heads. Blanche walked out into the field and asked my mother if she was interested in a new line of work. She didn't have to ask twice.

My mother left the next day, leaving me and Patricia behind. That's how I came to live with my grandmother.

My mother's brothers and sisters actually wanted to put me in an orphanage, but my grandmother wouldn't have it. They tried to convince her to keep

Patricia and get rid of me. The men were especially persistent since they all had had run-ins with Buddy, and Buddy didn't lose any fights. They just hated anything that had his blood in it, especially a son that looked just like him. I know they're not going to like seeing that in print, but it's the truth. Plus I was sick all the time. I had chicken pox, measles, the mumps, you name it. Nobody ever wanted to hold me because they were afraid they'd get sick.

But my grandmother, Birdie Lee Collins Watson, wouldn't let them put me in that home. She moved away from the rest of the family and got a place on North 15th Street on the outskirts of Corsicana. It was a two-story house without running water—we used an outhouse in the back—and we shared three little rooms while Grandma rented out the other half of the house. It was just fine for me and Grandma.

Patricia stayed with us occasionally, but mostly she was passed around among my aunts and uncles in town. I saw her at school more than I saw her at home.

My grandma—I called her momma until many years later—had long black hair down to her butt and the tired face of a woman who had raised six children with barely enough money to feed them. She wasn't ugly, but she dipped snuff and had more important things to worry about than how she looked. My grandfather had already passed on, so my grandma lived entirely off her old-age pension. We didn't have some basic things, like a radio or an icebox, but grandma found ways to provide. When I was a baby, she would feed me by straining pinto bean soup through rags since I couldn't nurse. And, later, when I was a boy, she bought packages of lard that came with a pill of yellow food coloring. You popped the pill and mixed it in with the lard until it looked like butter, then spread it on toast. Believe it or not, that was my favorite meal, mainly because grandma sometimes let me do the mixing.

It was a working house, even for us kids. I'd do women's work like churning butter and milking cows at our next-door neighbors, the Higginbothams, just so I could bring a little something back home. Everybody had to do little stuff like that. From the time I was seven, I worked the cotton fields each summer. I didn't actually pick cotton because the crop wasn't ready in the summer—my job was what we called choppin' cotton, which basically means keeping the weeds out of the plants. It burned me up that Patricia never had to chop cotton like me. They brought her out one time, and she couldn't stay within the rows. Instead of following one row at a time, she moved sideways across the field. To this day I'm not sure if that was evidence of how smart she is, or how dumb, but either way she never joined us out there again.

It was a simple life, and a good one in many ways, but it wasn't easy and grandma didn't let me and Patricia think otherwise. There is no Santa Claus, she told us as soon as we could understand, nor anyone else likely to give you something for nothing. But she was not bitter. In fact, I never heard my grandmother say a negative word. Whenever we'd complain, she'd always come back with some funny little saying. I'd say, "Momma, I'm hungry." And she'd say, "Well, tighten that belt up another notch."

Her philosophy was simple: Be honest, work hard, and don't complain. There were other people worse off than us, she said, and we should be grateful for the blessings we have. That simple country wisdom is all my grandma had to offer me. She knew she wasn't going to be around as I grew into a man, so she made sure I understood those things as a young boy.

Grandma also introduced me to Jesus, indirectly anyway. Like most small towns in those days, it seemed like there were more churches than people in Corsicana. I think people need the Lord more when they live off the land, or at least feel like they do. They prayed for the right weather to allow them to feed their families. And it seemed like everybody had five or six kids, because having a bunch of kids meant plenty of free labor. So then they had to pray about how to manage all those damn kids.

There was a little one-room church down the street—the Church of the Nazarene, it was called—and my grandmother walked me down there every Sunday morning. She'd get within about fifty yards and then tell me to go on in by myself. I don't know why she never went, but the whole time I lived with her she never darkened the door of a church. Her husband died young, and maybe she was mad at God about that. I'm not sure, but she made sure I went.

I enjoyed church. I liked talking to God and knowing that he would answer my prayers, at least sometimes. It always felt right to me. I even enjoyed studying the Bible. During Sunday school, the teachers would quiz us on Bible verses and give us a gold star for each correct answer. For some reason, they would place the stars across our forehead, probably so all the adults would know which kids were learning the Bible and which ones were throwing spit-wads and acting up. I usually did pretty well, and I'd go home in the afternoon with a row of stars across my forehead. Ever since then, even during my wild years, I've always read the Bible each day. I once wrote a song called "Ride Me Down Easy"—Bobby Bare took it to number one on the country charts—and I referred to myself as "a hobo with stars in my crown." That description fits me still.

Though I loved Jesus, I was still a crazy little kid. I had my share of adventures chasing snakes, playing in the creeks, and roughhousing with the boys in the neighborhood. It's amazing I was never seriously hurt, considering all the dumb things I did back then. My only close call was once when I was riding a friend's bicycle down the street, and a car came screaming around a corner and knocked me flying. I was bleeding like a stuck pig and had scrapes all over my body when I stumbled back home. My Uncle Joyce, a notoriously lazy person, was standing there with a cigar in his mouth ironing clothes and singing "Some Enchanted Evening." He took one look at me and said, "Boy, you look like a bear got a hold of you."

The ladies that ran over me followed me home and took me to the hospital. When I got there, a black boy was waiting to see the doctor too. He had been trying to tag along with his brothers on the way into town, and snuck onto the running board of their car before they took off. Since his brothers didn't know he was there, they took a corner real fast and threw him off, which chewed him up like ground meat. I thought I was in bad shape but he looked much worse. The doctor came to look me over but I told him I was okay—he should check out the black boy first. That's the way it worked back then, but I knew he needed help more than I did.

The doctor couldn't find any broken bones or anything on me. He just told me to go stand in what looked like a shower and close my eyes. He doused me with mercurochrome, which stung like hell and turned my skin a strange red color for about the next three months.

More than anything, I loved to sing. I'd do my own versions of the songs I heard around, like "Pins and Needles in My Heart" and "The Great Speckled Bird." During the day I crossed the railroad tracks and hung out with the black folks on their front yards and porches. There was always a slide guitar, and I learned a lot of the old blues songs there. A few times, when we were short, my grandmother took me down to the general store when she asked for an extension on her credit.

"Yeah, I'll give you an extension if you get that boy to sing," the lady said from behind the counter.

I thought it was for real. I thought I was really singing for my supper, so I'd get up on that cracker barrel and just sing my heart out. At night, my grandmother would sit on the front porch dipping her snuff and tell me I was going to be on the Grand Ole Opry someday. She was right, though it took me almost sixty years.

One night, I even came face to face with Hank Williams. I was old enough to read, so it was probably sometime in the late 1940s. I'd seen signs around town for a concert by Homer and Jethro and the Light Crust Doughboys at the Wonder Bread factory. All the kids liked Homer and Jethro because they sang those old corny songs that were pretty funny, but I thought they were incredible players too. After grandma went to bed, I opened the window and climbed out into the backyard. Patricia woke up and threatened to tell Grandma but I knew she wouldn't.

Like everyone else's, our outhouse was behind the main house. Every couple of weeks, a wagon came through and emptied them all out—we called it the honeywagon. The honeywagon carved a trail through the bushes and the weeds behind our house and I followed that trail until I got to the railroad tracks, where I balanced my little feet on the beams and headed toward town. When I got to the trestles, I walked between the beams to stay as far away as possible from the hobos who curled up in there to sleep.

At the Wonder Bread factory they let me in free—I guess because I was just a kid—and I saw all the musicians up on the loading docks and the crowd standing around in the hole where the trucks parked. Corsicana was a dry town, but the bootleggers were doing good business down in that pit that night.

I shimmied up a pole so I could see and so I wouldn't get my feet stepped on. Homer and Jethro were just finishing up, and they made an announcement that they were going to let a young man sing who they thought was going to be a big star. I know during those days Hank used to go around performing as Luke the Drifter, but they introduced him that night as Hank Williams. He had on a suit and a hat, and he looked really spiffy. He only did one song, and most of the crowd wasn't listening because they'd never heard of him. But Hank saw me up on that pole and just fixated on me with this hard stare, probably because I was the only one paying attention. He sang right straight to me, and it was lonesome and sad and beautiful all wrapped up together.

When I got home, my grandma heard me come through the window and she whupped me with a switch until I was plum wore out. You remember a whooping like that, and that's another reason my memories of that night are so clear.

FOR MOST OF MY CHILDHOOD, I only saw my mother once or twice a year. Sometimes she came on Christmas, but not always. But even on those visits she never showed me much affection. She never hugged me, and that tore me up, but I know now that she just didn't yet know how to be a mother.

But when I was six, I got to spend the summer in Waco. My grandmother must have really needed a break. But instead of staying with my mother, I stayed with Emma Jean, a fat black woman who cooked at the Green Gables for Blanche. Emma Jean and I spent our afternoons at a tank next to the General Tire plant where we fished for perch with her old cane pole. My skinny little butt and her big fat butt sitting by that pond must have made quite a sight. At night, we played music on her front porch. Her son, who was blind, was about my age and played the stand-up piano like a house a-fire. He'd play and I'd sing, and we'd carry on for hours at a time.

Some afternoons, I hung out at the Green Gables, though I was under orders not to bother my mother or call her "Momma" or anything else that would let on that I was her kid. The Green Gables was a wood-frame building with swinging screen doors and a big, wide dance floor covered with cornmeal so the couples could slide around while they danced. The jukebox in the corner played country acts like Jimmie Rodgers and the Carter Family, but also blues singers and popular artists of the day. It was on Highway 6 southeast of Waco on the way to Perry, which was the only town in the area where you could buy liquor. That highway stayed busy as a one-eyed dog in a smokehouse. They just served beer and set-ups at the Green Gables, but you could bring in a bottle you bought in Perry, or you could buy a slug of booze off of one of the bootleggers for a nickel or something. It was the mid-forties, and there were lots of bases in Central Texas at that time, so there were lots of military folks in and out of there, too.

Blanche inherited the place from a previous marriage, one of several that ended with a funeral. She was a voluptuous blonde woman, and she turned the heads of all the guys that came through the doors. She kept the rings from all of her dead husbands and they covered her fingers.

One day—and I remember this as clear as day—I was hanging on to the end of the bar listening to Blanche and my mother.

"Tincie, there's gonna be an old boy come up here in a few hours," Blanche said. "He's gonna be a rich 'un, with one foot in the grave and the other on a nanner peel. And I'm gonna nail his ass to the wall."

It wasn't less than two hours later that this fella floated up in a baby-blue Cadillac. He wore a floppy hat, and he took it off in the parking lot and wiped the sweat off his brow. Maybe I imagined it, but it was like he was trying to figure out what force drew him to this broke-down roadhouse on the edge of town. He hung around for a couple of weeks and sure enough Blanche got another ring for her collection. It wasn't too much later that fella had his funeral.

Between the regulars and the military folks, I got plenty of attention at the Green Gables. I guess I reminded those soldiers of their kids, so they would grab me and throw me up in the air and give me nickels. Sometimes they would throw me so high I'd hit the ceiling, and it felt great. I'd have a pocketful of nickels at the end of each day. Sometimes they'd let me put one of my nickels in the jukebox, and it seemed like it would play forever.

WHEN I WAS TWELVE, my grandmother died. I'm not sure what the cause was—I think she just wore out. My memories of that time are not clear, which is strange because I always knew she loved me more than anyone in the world—and I loved her just as much. But I don't remember who told me she died, or seeing her lying in the casket. I just remember being in the house the day of the funeral, and all the relatives were over claiming furniture and utensils and anything else they could use in their homes. I was sitting on the floor in a corner and eventually everybody left, including my mother and Patricia, and I was there by myself. They finally came and got me the next day.

No one was really sure what to do with me. My aunts and uncles, of course, didn't want to take me in, which left either my father or my mother.

I'd only seen my father once since I was born, and let's just say we didn't exactly bond. I was about five, and he was over at my Aunt Vinny's. If my grandma had known Buddy was over there she would've never let me go, but somehow she didn't know.

By this time Buddy was married to another woman—her name was Elizabeth, but everyone called her Lizzie. She was full-blooded Indian with shiny black hair and a temper to match my father's. According to the stories I heard later, they used to take off to Dallas for a few weeks at a time and come back with wads of cash. People said they were a regular Bonnie and Clyde. My father always carried a gun, while Lizzie carried a long switch-blade knife in her purse. They were a good team and they stayed together until the end.

The day I went to Aunt Vinny's, I met him in the living room.

"Yeah, kid, I'm your dad," he said, looking down at me with a crooked grin.

That's all he said. My half-sister, Wanda Jean, was there in a pretty pink dress—she was Buddy's favorite, and he doted on her and pretty much ignored me. But late that day he walked me out in the backyard, where he grabbed these two old cats, tied their tails together and threw them over a clothesline. They just tore each other to pieces. It was a mean-ass thing to do, but he was testing me. He wanted me to watch it, while he just laughed like crazy.

But I started crying, which made him mad. I tried to run away, and he chased me around the yard. I wanted to get out of there, and I grabbed Wanda Jean's hand to bring her with me. When we turned a corner on the side of the house, she fell sideways into a big basket of tomatoes. She was covered in tomato juice, and I guess he thought she was bleeding because he came after me even faster. But I was real skinny and I could run a hole in the wind. He never caught me, but I believe he'd a killed me if he had. I ran straight home, and that's the last time I saw him for about twelve years.

So eventually my mother took me to Waco with her and Patricia. I guess she didn't really have much choice.

chapter two

Ain't No God in Mexico

□

Ain't no God in Mexico
Ain't no way to understand
How that border-crossin' feelin'
Makes a fool out of a man
If I'd never felt the sunshine
I would not curse the rain
If my feet could fit a railroad track
I guess I'd a been a train.

I WAS A SWEET LITTLE BOY, but I'll be the first to admit I wasn't a particularly nice young man. I was twelve years old when I moved to Waco, just starting to become a man. There was a part of me that was excited about the possibility of getting to know my mother for the first time, but the timing wasn't right: My mother was growing out of her rebellious phase just as I was growing into mine.

By the time I showed up in Waco, Tincie had found her way out of the honky tonks and was working as a regular waitress at Leslie's Chicken Shack on Interstate 35. She had married a mechanic and we lived in a two-bedroom house. Patricia stayed in the spare bedroom, and I slept on the couch. We were not in Waco proper, but Bellmead, a working-class suburb north of Waco not far from the James Connolly Air Force Base.

My mother started going to church again. My stepfather, a Czechoslovakian named Adolph Joseph Mach, didn't go with her—he was an atheist—but he was a good man, all in all. He provided for my mother and treated her right, but he and I never could get along.

It's hard for a man to raise another man's son, and he lost me early on when he gave away my guitar. It was a little Gene Autry guitar my grandmother gave me before she died. Well, one day Adolph hired this Mexican man to dig a stump out of our yard, and the man brought his little boy with him. When they were done, Adolph gave my guitar to the Mexican boy. He was punishing me for something, I can't remember what, but I never forgave him for that.

A boy without a father picks up on things wherever he can, and I guess I got most of my early life lessons from James French. He was my cousin by marriage, and I followed him around Corsicana like a puppy for the last two years I was there. He was a lot older than me—he was about fifteen then, I think—and he spent most of his time either fighting or fucking. He fought everybody in town it seemed like, and, while I don't know what kind of lover he was, the girls sure seemed to like him. James never let anybody hurt me, and he was the closest thing I had to a good friend my age. After I moved to Waco, I got word that he'd killed himself playing Russian roulette.

So when I started seventh grade in Waco, at La Vega, I did a pretty fair James French impression—at least the fighting part. I was real skinny and the other boys picked on me a lot, but I started my share of tussles too. I got a reputation as a little outlaw.

I worked at Leslie's washing dishes and spent more time there than I did at school. After a couple of months, the owner, Leslie Blanton, offered me a job as a busboy making twenty dollars a week. He tried to make it sound like a promotion, since I'd be getting out of the kitchen, but I knew he would just work me longer hours and never pay me overtime, so I quit and went back to school. But school wasn't a good fit for me either, never was.

I had a bad attitude toward school ever since the first grade because they made me repeat it. What happened was my sister Patricia got held back in the second grade that year, and if they had let me move up we would have been in the same grade. Patricia threw a fit about it and started crying and complaining to Grandma. She talked it over with the principal, and they decided it would be best to keep us both back for one more year, which made me mad as hell.

I didn't get anything out of school again until I met Ms. Legg when I was in seventh grade.

Ms. Legg taught twelfth grade English literature, so she wasn't my every-day teacher, but we had a period each day called homeroom, which was really more of a study period. The teachers from all the grades rotated in and out, and most of them just sat there while we pretended to study. But Ms. Legg always gave us little assignments. One day she asked us to write a poem, and I did it, and then she asked us again the next time she was in homeroom. When I turned mine in, she said, "Did you get these somewhere else?"

"You told us to write 'em, so I wrote 'em," I told her. I was trying to be a little tough guy.

But she didn't believe me, so I said, "You tell me what to write about, and I'll write you another one."

"Write one about outer space," she replied.

I came back the next day with a poem about space that really knocked her out. She asked me if she could put it in the school yearbook, and I said she could, but only if she didn't put my name on it. Back in those days, you were considered a sissy for playing music, much less writing poetry. But Ms. Legg made sure I understood I had a gift as a writer.

"It's just something I do," I said. "I've been doing it a while."

"You've got talent, and you can always fall back on that. As long as you are honest with what you write, you will always have something special to say," she told me.

Ms. Legg's encouragement meant the world to me. She was the first person that ever read my writing, and she liked it. She knew I had something to say, and she tried to make sure I had the confidence to say it.

From then on, she always stopped me in the halls and asked me if I was writing, and I always said I was, even if I wasn't. She was the only teacher that gave a darn about me.

Most of the others just saw me as a punk. In eighth grade, I showed up to school with a Cherokee strip—most people today call it a Mohawk. The principal expelled me right away, which was fine with me, except I thought I could still play football. But the coach didn't like my new look either: "You go shave that fuckin' head of yours and then go talk to the principal," he growled. "Then maybe I'll let you play some football."

He put me back on the team but that was about it for me. Later that year, Ms. Legg got wind that I was dropping out. She came to talk me out of it.

"Ms. Legg, I got a lot of living to do and I can't do it here," I explained.

Ms. Legg started to argue, but then she thought about it a while. All she said to me was, "Do what you think is right."

I quit going to school right after that.

Tincie and Adolph weren't getting along about then, and he convinced my mother that I was coming between them. They got along fine before I got there, he said, and I suspect he was right.

So I started staying away from home more and more. There was a hobo jungle behind my mother's house, and at night I'd sit around back with the hoboes while they cooked wild chickens and told stories about hopping trains and traveling around the country. It sounded pretty exciting, and pretty soon I was wandering further and further from home. At first I explored other neighborhoods in town, then I moved on to other little towns nearby, and next thing you know

I was staying gone for days at a time. My mother and stepfather didn't seem to notice I was gone.

Most of my adventures were solitary ones. It was easier to travel that way, and most of the boys I knew couldn't stay gone that long without getting in serious trouble. When I was on the road, I did odd jobs at service stations to make a few bucks to get me to the next town. I slept on the ground under the stars and it never bothered me a bit. I hitchhiked to Arizona one time, and another time I almost got to California. A couple of hoboes told me I could get a job in the movies out there, and so I talked some other kids into going with me. Instead of hitchhiking, we took an old beat-up car that barely ran, but it broke down in Arizona. That's about when the other boys got homesick, so we sold the car for thirty dollars in parts. They gave me five dollars and went back to Waco. I stuck around and got a job gathering peaches in an orchard, but never made it to California.

In every town I went through, I checked the phone book for my father's name. Years later, Merle Haggard sang a song about doing that, and when I heard it, I thought, "Damn, that song is about me." I'd never heard anything good about my father but I still wanted to know him. It's not that I felt a void in my life or anything as major as that. I just wanted to know who he was. I think every man wants to know his father.

As it happened, I learned about the world on my own, for better and for worse. I learned how to make a buck and how to stay alive on the road, and, slowly but surely, I learned a thing or two about women. My first experience with women as sexual creatures came with my Aunt Louise. We were in Corsicana—I wasn't more than eight—and Louise took me downtown with a friend of hers, a black girl. (Louise always liked black folks more than white folks and she later married a black man.) We were at the train depot, and Louise and her friend took me into the ladies room with them. The black girl cocked her leg up on the toilet. She didn't have anything on under her dress.

"Looky there, Bubba, you know what that is?" Louise asked. (Most people called me Bubba when I was little.)

"It looks like a crow with a red ribbon in it's mouth," I said.

They fell out laughing. To this day, I'm not sure if they just wanted a good laugh or if they had something else in mind. But my grandmother heard about it and she wouldn't let me be alone with Louise from then on.

So between Louise and James French I had a general idea of how the parts fit together between a man and a woman. That's about it.

Then, in Waco, I ran around with these boys who swore that the first girl I slept with had to be a black girl or else I wasn't a true Texan. I wasn't going to let anyone question my status as a true Texan, so I marched over to Elm Street in East Waco one night with five other guys. There were about a half-dozen buildings where a guy could get that sort of thing taken care of back then, so we chose one and stood in line. The woman called us in one after the other. She laid there on her side and I handed her two dollars—about a day's work at Leslie's—and climbed on. In less than thirty seconds, she pushed me off and said, "You're done."

It amazed me how quickly a man could become a true Texan. I told her I didn't think I was done, but she was bigger than me and so I left. I was glad it was over and the thought of trying it again didn't cross my mind until several years later.

WHEN I WAS FOURTEEN, I almost died for the first time. I was out gathering snakes near Asa, a little town outside of Waco, with a friend of mine named Shelby. He was several years older than me, and we were in his car. Shelby kept the snakes and used them in a show he gave for kids at school. I was just along for the ride.

Late in the afternoon it started to rain, so we decided to head back to town. We came to an S-curve in the road, and Shelby lost control of the car. We plowed into a pole by the side of the road. The car wrapped around it so tight the front and back of the car were practically touching. I flew through the windshield and landed on a set of railroad tracks. When I touched my head, all I could feel was skull. I was just about scalped. Shelby also got thrown from the car but he was barely scratched.

The first car that came along was full of black kids in gowns and tuxedoes, so I guess they were on their way to the prom. They took off running as soon as they saw my head. The next person was a nice white lady dressed in a fancy fur coat. She wrapped me in her coat and promised to drive me to the hospital. I apologized for bleeding all over her coat, but she didn't seem to mind.

Before we could leave, an ambulance arrived. The geniuses who showed up bumped my head getting in and out of the ambulance, so I think I would have been better off staying with the lady. Anyway, at the hospital they shaved my head and reattached my scalp with 136 stitches. For the next week, I sat in a rocking chair and barely moved. I was in so much pain. I slowly recovered and eventually the hair grew back, but it came in grey on the sides in a way that made it look like I colored it. Years later, once I got married, I had my wife color my hair so it looked natural. I didn't want people to think I was a phony.

When I was fifteen, I got word that a trucking company in South Texas was looking for drivers to take gasoline trucks out to California. I took the job even though I didn't know how to drive an eighteen-wheeler. But I learned quickly enough. While going down a four-mile grade in Arizona, I got stuck between gears and just about burned up the brakes trying to stop the truck. I thought about jumping out but knew that would be suicide. I fish-tailed down the highway and almost ran over every car in my path. At the bottom of the hill, I finally got the truck geared down and pulled over in the sand. I immediately got out of the truck with my little bag and started hitchhiking back toward Texas before the rest of the convoy got to the bottom of the hill.

The wrangler for the trucking company pulled up in his limo and said, "Hey, boy, get back over in that truck."

"I ain't getting back in that truck," I said. "I'm going back to Texas."

"You don't know how to drive a truck, do you?" he said.

"I do now," I said.

He saw that I meant business and offered me a $1 more per hour to finish the trip. I almost didn't take it, but I figured I at least knew how to drive now so I might as well finish the job.

I became friends with two other drivers, Daniel Garza and Juan Rodriguez, who barely spoke English. We couldn't understand each other about half the time, but we got along great and I later moved into a little trailer with them in Santa Maria, California. One of our first conversations was at a pit stop where Juan pulled me aside. "Why do they prosecute the little bugs?" he asked. "They don't prosecute the big bugs?"

I couldn't figure out what the hell he was talking about.

"The sign say, 'Little bugs will be prosecuted. Why? Are they afraid of the big bugs?'" he asked.

I laughed 'til I thought my sides were gonna split. "It's litter bugs, Juan, not little bugs," I said.

Our job in California was to fuel the planes for all the pilots at Vandenberg Air Force Base. We made very little money, so we did what we could to survive. As soon as the pilots took off, we loaded up on the leftover doughnuts, cans of cream, biscuits, and what ever else they left behind. Many days that was the only thing we ate.

We did manage to get drunk on a regular basis, even if it was on Thunderbird and cheap tequila. Since we didn't eat much it didn't take long for us to get a good buzz on. We spent many nights terrorizing Santa Maria.

One night I brought a gal home to our trailer and took her in the back room. I did everything I could think of with her, and a few things she thought of. Then Juan started beating on the door and wanted a turn, and she said she was up for it.

Out in the other room, Daniel was pouring coal oil in the stove and complaining that he couldn't get it to light. At the same time, Juan was building up steam and rocking the trailer pretty good. It started to roll down the hill, which was our fault because we never put the trailer on blocks like we should have. The roof was covered with tar and it somehow caught fire from all the oil Daniel poured in the stove. Daniel and I jumped out and watched this ball of fire slide between two other trailers before it finally came to rest. Juan and the girl jumped out naked just as the trailer rolled to a stop, which was quite a spectacle.

The old guy who owned the trailer park told us we needed to move out the next day. So we quit our jobs at the base the next day and bought an old run-down car for eighty dollars. It took us three days to get it to start but we headed back to Texas, where we moved in with Daniel's parents at their home in Harlingen.

Every night the three of us walked across the border to check out the bars in Matamoros. Not surprisingly, I eventually got arrested, though surprisingly, it wasn't for fighting—I got drunk and started throwing bottles around a bar.

The Mexican police wore me out with a power hose and then threw me in a tiny cell by myself. They called my parents to try to get some money out of them, but my stepfather wouldn't go my bail. I was in there for about a week. I managed to hide a few bucks on my person before they shook me down.

Most of the other prisoners didn't speak English, but the guy in the next cell understood me one day when I asked him for a cigarette.

"It'll cost you a dollar," he said.

I gave him a dollar and he passed the cigarette over to me.

"Hey, man," I said, "pass me a match."

"Cost you a dollar."

So I gave him another one and he sent over the match. Before I could strike it, he said, "Don't strike it on the wall—you need to use a special surface for the match to work." It was a safety match, so I had to pay another dollar for the striker to light the match.

That damned cigarette cost me three dollars, and ruined any good feelings I had left about Mexico. "This a bad place to be," I thought to myself. "Ain't no God in this place."

My song, "Ain't No God in Mexico," which Waylon Jennings recorded on *Honky Tonk Heroes*, is based on that week of my life.

Finally, Daniel and Juan sold the car to raise money to get me out of jail. It was an especially generous thing to do considering they apparently had made up their minds that they didn't want anything more to do with me. They came and picked me up in a pickup truck they borrowed from an uncle, drove across the border, and dropped me on the side of the highway pointed north to Waco. They'd brought all my clothes with them and everything. "Adios, loco gringo," Juan said as they drove off.

WHEN I GOT BACK TO WACO, I decided to join the Navy and convinced my best friend, Larry Smith, to go with me. At least I thought I did. I told my mother, and she thought that sounded like a pretty good place for me, and so the day after Larry and I made our decision I went and signed up. Later that day, though, I saw Larry and asked him when he was shipping out. He wasn't. He just had his eye on the same girl I did, and he figured his chances were better if I was out of the way.

It was 1956, and it was the day I turned seventeen when they sent me to San Diego for boot camp. Elvis was in the airport that day, and I got to shake his hand. After boot camp, they sent me to Illinois to train for the hospital corps, and then I was assigned to the base in Portsmouth, Virginia, where I worked at the Portsmouth Naval Hospital.

We had some good times—drinking, fighting, and getting laid whenever we could—but mostly we watched people die. Our ward was designated for terminal patients, so we didn't do much other than try to make them comfortable. I learned to change IVs and run a bunch of tests, but I spent most of my time just talking to the patients and getting in trouble.

I made the mistake one night of calling a group of black sailors "niggers," and that was maybe the only time I've ever run from a fight in my life. I knew I'd done the wrong thing, so I took my medicine and let these fellas beat the tar out of me for a few minutes. I didn't even fight back. When I got a chance, I took off running and hid under a bed in a dormitory. They found me, of course, but before they could start wailing on me again, an enormous black man came out of nowhere and told them to leave me alone. They explained what I'd said, but he answered: "You touch him, you answer to me." He was like an angel that came down from heaven to save me, 'cause I never saw him again.

I guess I should explain myself: I knew better than to use that word, but I'd grown up with it. In the South back then there were certain people who taught kids to hate, and they were good at it. When I got to Waco, I stopped hanging around black folks as much and started to use the language that I heard around me, even though I knew it was hurtful to blacks. It's a poor excuse to say I didn't know any better. My point is that children don't hate other people naturally—they learn to hate when adults tell them they should, and too many adults back then convinced their white children to hate black people. We're better now, but we've still got quite a ways to go.

Not long after that, I went AWOL to visit my old friend from Waco, Larry Smith, who finally joined the Army when he couldn't corral that girl. He was a paratrooper in Cherry Point, North Carolina. When I got down there, Larry stashed me in an old warehouse until he could find the right time to leave. He brought me fruits and snacks so I wouldn't starve, and after a few days he brought me a set of old clothes because mine were so nasty. We finally snuck out one night and caught a ride right away—everybody picked up soldiers in those days. We stopped off at a gas station to clean up in the bathroom, but we made a mistake: we stayed in there for about fifteen minutes but didn't buy anything. That made the owner mad, and he called the police. Next thing I knew, I was in the stockade in Camp Stewart, Georgia.

It was rainy and muddy and we stayed in tents that were impossible to keep clean. It was really miserable, and I was dying to get back to my base, but I couldn't convince the Army that I was in the Navy. The guy running the place thought I was a paratrooper since I was wearing the uniform when I got caught. He was a black guy and could tell I was a bit of a bigot, and I could tell he was, too. We knocked heads for two weeks until he finally got orders to send me back to Portsmouth Naval Hospital, Virginia. When he put me on a train back to Portsmouth, he handcuffed me to this muscled black fella going the same direction. He probably thought we'd kill each other before we got across the state line, and we almost did. When the guards turned their heads, I'd punch him or he'd elbow me. We battled like that for hours. Finally, we both just wore out and started talking to each other instead of fighting. It was the first time since I was a boy that I'd talked with a black person, and it felt right to me. That trip took me back to what I'd known as a boy, and what I'd always known in my heart—that people of all kinds are about the same. There's some good ones and some bad ones, and the goodness doesn't have anything to do with skin color.

EVERY SIX MONTHS, we got to go on leave. I usually found a place nearby to get rowdy for a few days, but I went back home once, and while I was there my Aunt Vinny let slip that she'd heard my father was living in Dallas. I decided to go see him. Why? That's hard to say. All the stories I'd heard about him made him out to be an evil person. The entire time I was growing up, whenever I misbehaved, somebody would say, "You're just like your sorry old daddy." I wanted to know him for myself.

I showed up on his porch late one afternoon in my Navy whites. He opened the door and it was like looking in the mirror.

"I'll be damned," he said. "Come on in."

We sat on the couch and shared a bottle of whiskey for most of the night. He wasn't a bad guy, but we didn't become long-lost pals either. He told me about his life, how he lived in California for a while and drove trucks for a while. In Dallas, he scavenged old cars and resold them. I told him how I got in the Navy and that my mother remarried. He didn't have much nice to say about her, but I cut him off because I didn't want to hear any of that.

He was still with Elizabeth, and they had matching souped-up Fords. He loved to drive fast. The next day, he drove me over to East Texas to meet his kinfolks, including my Aunt Billy, who I was named after.

The next year, when I got out of the Navy, I went back to Dallas and lived with him and Elizabeth for a couple of weeks. It didn't go well. He said some nasty things about my mother, and the last day I was there we ended up brawling in his front yard among all the beat-up cars he kept there.

I only saw him one other time. It was the late 1960s, and I was coming through Dallas playing a gig. Somebody got word to me that he was dying of heart failure in the hospital, the end result from a lifetime of whiskey and cigarettes. He was my father and for that reason I loved him, but I didn't feel sad about him dying. I just said good-bye. I didn't owe him much but at least I owed him that. He was fifty-six, I think.

BACK TO THE NAVY. Like I said, I couldn't stay out of trouble—even when it wasn't my fault. The final straw was when I was at a party and got sucker-punched in the back of the head, knocked flat on my face. When I turned over, I kicked the guy in the balls and then stood up and decked him. The base police showed up and I fought them, too, and they eventually caught me and threw the book at me: resisting arrest, destruction of government property, and assaulting an officer. But it turns out the guy who punched me—an off-duty officer—confused me with another guy who was running around with his girlfriend. I was facing a dishonorable discharge, so I wrote a letter to the commandant of the Fifth Naval District explaining my situation. He arranged for a top-notch Marine lawyer to defend me at the court martial, and the jury found me not guilty.

I wanted to stay in the Navy but the commander didn't think that was such a good idea.

"I used to love the fisticuffs myself, son, and I know your type: you're never going to let anybody tell you what to do," he said.

He was right. Ever since my grandmother died, I'd never listened to anybody. I took my honorable discharge and went home to Waco.

chapter three

Fit to Kill
and Going Out in Style

□

My woman is the queen of the world
She ain't just an ordinary girl
She makes country lovin' like an oyster makes a pearl
I'm gonna let her hold my heart a while

We're the talk of the town every night
We do our thing until the morning light
We're a head above the highbrows by a money-makin' mile
We're fit to kill and going out in style

BRENDA TINDELL WAS TALL AND SKINNY, but shapely, with long hair like my grandmother's and the prettiest smile you've ever seen. She played basketball at Connolly High School, and I met her when I was at a football game with one of her teammates, Peggy Hill. Brenda was a senior in high school, and I was twenty and just out of the Navy.

It was bitter cold, and I was wearing a long heavy jacket. During the game, I felt the back of it rise up and a set of toes wiggle around underneath the coat. I turned around and Brenda pulled her feet back, kind of embarrassed, but I told her it was okay. She was just keeping her feet warm. Peggy saw us talking and introduced us. That was it for me—love at first sight, the whole thing.

I saw her again a couple of days later at the Greyhound bus station, where I was hanging out with a bunch of other hoods. We used to go down there and stand around smoking cigarettes, trying to look cool in our motorcycle jackets even though none of us could afford a motorcycle. I looked over one day and saw Brenda getting put on a bus by her father. I found out later she was going to stay with her uncle for a while at his watermelon farm near Lockhart. We made eye contact but neither of us said a word that day.

When she got back, I ran into her downtown one night and set up a double date with my friend, Larry Smith, and his girlfriend. We drove out to the lake near the Bosque River and Larry parked. He was in the front with his girl, and she wouldn't fool around with him while we were in the car so he made us get out. There was a little boarded-up shack not far from where we parked. I took Brenda in there and laid her down. We didn't say much, but we made love there on the floor. From then on she was my girl. I knew I wasn't her first man—in fact, she was dating a couple of other guys when she first went out with me. But that didn't bother me—she wasn't my first woman either. I thought the sun rose and set on her. She was the most beautiful thing I'd ever seen and she knew it. She liked to ride horses in her bikini and I rode along next to her, following her every move. It felt right to me from the very beginning.

I borrowed Larry's car and took her out as often as I could. She loved going out for pickles. Within a couple of weeks of our first date, she told me she was pregnant. She graduated from high school without anyone knowing except me and her. We talked about eloping but her dad was planning to give her a brand-new Corvette for finishing school.

"Baby, don't you want that Corvette?" I asked. It was a beautiful car. But she said, "I only want you."

So we drove up to Hillsboro, the justice of the peace's wife played a little song on the piano, and we got married. It was a glorious thing, the start of a forty-year love affair that lasted until she died. We had lots of ups and downs along the way—hell, we divorced twice and got married three times. She always gave as good as she got. She was high-spirited, and she wasn't perfect, but I never loved another woman the way I loved Brenda.

I worked at Cameron Mills, a local sawmill, and we settled in a little rent house near the mill. I didn't make much money, but we were young and in love. Our son Eddy was born June 20, 1962, and he just added to our happiness. I walked to the mill each morning and rushed home at night to play with my new son. Unfortunately, Brenda's dad wasn't too happy about the situation. He didn't like me and he knew I'd been in fights all over town. Not long after we married, he came over to the house and pulled a knife on me. He told me he was taking Brenda back home. I didn't want to fight Brenda's father so I stayed as calm as possible.

"Please leave, Mr. Tindell," I said. Whenever he said something else, I just repeated the same thing. "Please leave." It was a pretty tense moment, but he finally turned and left without violence. After that, he decided it was better to get along with me than risk losing his daughter for good.

Ed Tindell was a horse trader, car salesman, and all-around wheeler-dealer. Once he accepted our marriage, he set us up in one of his houses on his property near James Connolly Air Force Base and helped us get a little car. Then he found out I could ride horses and started working the shit out of me on my days off. It was the start of my cowboy period. I spent every weekend breaking horses, dehorning cattle, and any other kind of chore imaginable for him. Sometimes he would even wake me up in the middle of the night to help him do chores. Ed was one of those guys who would say, "We've got to do this and we've got to do that" and then *you* would be the one who ended up doing it. Worse, he never paid me in cash. He paid me with old tires and car parts and all sorts of stuff, so I ended up with a barn full of useless crap. One night he even asked me to go with him down to where a train loaded with feed derailed, and he filled up the truck with sacks of stolen feed. He wasn't a bad man, I don't think, but he had a touch of larceny in him, and we were at each other's throats quite a bit.

Ed was friends with a guy named Pat Patterson, who bought a ranch with all the money he made from inventing some sort of vending machine, and Ed hauled me out to Pat's place to help with the cattle on a regular basis. I wasn't the best cowboy in Central Texas, but I could relate to the animals better than a lot of them. I was especially good with the ornery ones that no one else could handle. We got called out to Pat's one day because this one bull was causing him all kinds of trouble—it was a big silver sucker, and you couldn't hardly get in the pen with him without him running you down. Slowly but surely, though, that bull got used to me and didn't bother me if I didn't get too close.

About this time, Ed and I got to arguing about the coat he was wearing. It was made of llama fur, and it had been left behind by an artist who passed through town. Ed didn't pay a dime for it, and I wanted it.

"What would it take for you to get rid of that coat?" I asked him.

"Ain't doing it," he said.

"I'll bet you a hundred dollars against that coat that I can kiss that bull on the mouth and walk off," I said.

Don't ask me how I came up with that brilliant idea.

"You're on," he said. "I've got to see this."

I walked right up and planted one on that bull, and I'll be damned if he didn't move the whole time. I collected the coat, and I wore that thing as proudly as any piece of clothing I've ever owned.

WHAT TIME I WASN'T DOING STUFF FOR ED, I was still working my main job at Cameron Mills. My job at the sawmill was to trim wooden doors—enormous doors so big you can't imagine why anyone would need them in the first place. The doors slid down a conveyor belt toward me, then I had to turn the doors and feed them into a machine called a double-end. I had to guide the doors into the pressure chains on the conveyor belt, and the chains, which held the door in place, looked like a caterpillar coming at you. On each side of the chain, there were large steel wheels about eight inches wide and five inches thick with razors in them going so fast you couldn't even see them. I had to guide the doors into the pressure chains just right or it would ruin them.

Well, one day we were in a hurry, and I let my mind wander a little bit. My first two fingers on my right hand got caught under the pressure chain that fed the doors down into those razors. I yanked on them but I couldn't get them loose in time. Sparks started flying, and I could feel the razors slicing through my fingers. There wasn't a safety switch, so I finally just put my feet up against the bottom of the belt and pushed off until they came loose.

I lost parts of three of my fingers, and the tendons and ligaments were stretched out and hanging down like wilted flowers. Strangely enough, I had just read an article in the newspaper about how surgeons in Japan discovered a way to reattach fingers and even get them to work again. So I crawled around in the sawdust under the belt and found the severed fingers. I carried them in my hand out to my pickup and drove myself to the doctor, a guy named Dr. Tabb.

Dr. Tabb was an old Navy doctor, a tall skinny guy, and some people said he had a bit of a drinking problem.

"Well, Billy," he said, "you got a little trouble here."

"I sure do," I said, and told him about the article I'd read. I thought he'd be able to put my fingers back together.

"Well, this ain't Japan. This is Waco, Texas," he said.

A young black nurse was there at Dr. Tabb's office, really cute and not more than twenty-five years old.

She asked me, "Mr. Billy, can I have them fingers?"

I guess I didn't really understand what she was saying, because I didn't answer and she had to ask me again. I told her she could have the fingers—I couldn't see how I would have much use for them. As she walked off, I asked her what she planned to do with them.

"I'm going to put them in a jar and keep them until the day I die," she said. She grabbed a mason jar off the shelf, filled it about half full of formaldehyde, and dropped the fingers in there. I always suspected she was going to use them for some sort of voodoo, and maybe she did. She may still be using them, for all I know.

At the hospital, Dr. Tabb trimmed the two fingers, leaving me with a stub just above the first knuckle on each finger, and took the top knuckle of my third finger. He did the best he could, I guess, but it looked like he could have done just as well with a hacksaw in somebody's woodshop behind the house.

When they wheeled me out, my little finger was still crooked and broken, so they had to wheel me back in for more surgery. Brenda told me I died on the operating table and they brought me back to life, though I don't know if that's true or not because I didn't see a bright light or anything like that. But to this day my pinkie finger hangs to the left real bad and isn't worth a damn. Over the next few days, I stayed in bed and thought about my life. Deep down, I'd always felt drawn to words and music, like that was what I was supposed to be doing. Maybe Ms. Legg was right. Maybe my true talent was as a writer. I had been writing songs and poems since I was five years old, and I had been singing songs all my life.

As I lay there in bed, my arm got infected and swelled up like a balloon. The doctor said if it didn't go down he was going to have to cut my arm off. I told my wife, my friends, and all the doctors and all the nurses: you cut my arm off and I will hunt you down and kill every single one of you. And I meant it, and Brenda knew it. To her credit, she stood firm and wouldn't let the doctors do it. I prayed to God and told him that I knew now what I should be doing. If you'll save my arm, I told Him, I'll do it—I'll go to work. I'll start writing songs. Sure enough, the swelling eventually went down.

Unfortunately, that wasn't my last encounter with Dr. Tabb. It was years later, when I was up in Nashville and I came back down to see Brenda (we were split up at the time). I drove ten hours down and went straight to bed as soon as I got to Waco.

"My stomach is killing me," I told Brenda.

She wasn't too sympathetic, since she knew the way I was living at the time. "It's probably all that dope you've been taking," she said.

"Naw, all I did was take some speed so I could stay awake to get down here," I said.

I begged Brenda to get me some Pepto Bismol, and I drank two big bottles in the span of an hour, but didn't feel any better. We called three or four doctors, and they all said we could come by the next day. I knew I wouldn't make it that long, and I decided to go to the emergency room. They figured out real quick that my appendix was hot and needed to come out right away. They shot me full of Demerol and said they would call out to the country club to get Dr. Tabb.

I was laying on a gurney feeling no pain when he finally showed.

"Hey, boy, thought I'd never see you again," he said, like we were old friends.

Then he started talking in graphic detail about what he was going to do—how he was going to cut me open and cut my appendix and scrape the gangrene out and on and on.

I said, "Hey, Doc, while you're down there, why don't you just circumcise me?"

I was just kidding around with him, and because of all the painkillers I thought it was pretty funny. But when I woke up after the operation, my stomach felt fine but I had a pain something fierce between my legs. I raised the sheets up, and, sure enough, there was a hunk of meat on the top of my penis with a ring of stitches all around it. I don't mean to be sacrilegious—nobody loves Jesus more than me—but I couldn't help but think it looked like my own little crown of thorns.

I couldn't do much but laugh, but Brenda was mad as hell because we couldn't make love for more than a month. When we finally got back in the swing of things, that little procedure seemed to help my performance somehow. She changed her tune after that. "I believe I'll call Dr. Tabb and thank him," she said.

AFTER I LOST MY FINGERS, I started writing a few songs here and there but still didn't really know how to make the next step. When I wasn't working for Ed, I spent most of my free time riding at rodeos and hitting the honky tonks with Brenda. I wasn't a particularly good cowboy, but I idolized the guys who were good at it. I was okay, but the truth is I had mainly had the gear and the attitude, but not enough talent. Brenda traveled with me to out-of-town rodeos, and she liked getting crazy as much as I did, but things were getting worse in our young marriage.

In about 1965, Ed died unexpectedly of a brain aneurysm. He was only forty-seven. That was tough on Brenda, and tougher on Mildred, Ed's wife. She was a good woman, and for a long time I thought of her as the mother I never really had. She understood that Brenda was headstrong and seemed to sympathize with my efforts to keep her in line.

Fortunately Ed left his family sitting pretty financially. I don't think Mildred knew Ed had that kind of money. But once she got control of it, it tore the family apart. Mildred thought I had designs on her money, when I couldn't care less. Brenda knew it, and my lack of greed made her mad. I couldn't win for losing. She had just about decided I was never going to amount to much—she sure didn't like this idea I had about becoming a songwriter. For my part, I suspected Brenda was running around on me.

I finally caught her one night after we went to see Merle Haggard at a club called the Night Owl. She spent most of the show dancing with another guy, a young kid named Terry. After the show, Terry walked out with me and Brenda, and I told him I had an errand to run and asked him if he would ride with me while Brenda followed behind in his car. We got in the truck, I turned on the overhead light, and then took my pistol out of my coat and laid it on the seat between us.

"You can go for the pistol, but one of us is going to die," I said. "Or you can tell me the truth: how long has this been going on?"

At first he denied it, then he admitted he'd been sleeping with her for about a week. Finally he came totally clean: they'd been having an affair for eleven months. I thought about blowing a hole in his head, but he was just a kid. It wasn't his fault.

I confronted Brenda at home, and she cried and told me how much she loved me. She said she thought I was all right with it, since I never got angry when she danced with other guys.

"I don't know any man who is okay with his wife sleeping with another man," I said.

I had to quit her, didn't really have a choice. I couldn't stay in Waco with everybody knowing what she'd done. It's a terrible thing to leave your wife and son, but I had to do it. Mildred had plenty of money to take care of Brenda and Eddy. So I moved to Dallas to sell cars for a while.

I joined a training program for car salesmen, but I never could sell a damn thing. They gave us a demo to drive home each night, and the only thing I was good at was wrecking those demos. It was a difficult time. Brenda was throwing parties and running around more than she was staying with Eddy—Mildred spent more time with Eddy back then than Brenda did—and I spent half my time going back and forth between Dallas and Waco. Once, on the way from Dallas to Waco, I woke up at the wheel of the car, going about ten miles an hour down the center of the median on Interstate 35. When I looked back, I saw from my tracks in the grass that I almost went into oncoming traffic but slid back down the hill just before I got to the top.

When I couldn't be with him, I called Eddy almost every night. Our relationship was always more friendly than like most fathers and sons. On weekends, we went to Six Flags over Texas, both of us dressed head-to-toe in Dallas Cowboys gear. He loved that place. At night, when they closed the park, they had to come find us or else we would have stayed all night.

Looking back, it was a real blessing that Mildred kept that money to herself. If she had given it to me and Brenda, I would have spent the rest of my life working for my mother-in-law, breaking horses and mending fences and everything else required to keep the ranch running. Instead, that became a productive time for me. I started writing songs—songs about my life and my feelings. I'm not going to say it was easy, but the words poured out of me, like they had been bottled up for too long.

Before long, I quit the car business and moved to Houston, which had more of a music scene back then. I started playing my songs at the Old Quarter and running with another young songwriter named Townes Van Zandt. He was about the hottest thing going, and I gained some confidence because I could tell my songs were about as good as his. There weren't many people as crazy as I was back then, but Townes was one of them, and we spent many nights getting drunk and making trouble around Houston.

Brenda and I got back together for a time, but the relationship really wasn't much better. For one, she hated Townes. She thought he was weird, which he was. I remember one time we went to pick up Townes, and when he got in the car he had teardrops painted on his face, like a clown.

"This is the last time I have anything to do with that crazy son-of-a-bitch," Brenda muttered. She also blamed him because every time we got together I came home liquored up. The truth is, I managed that just fine on my own. Still, I spent more and more time on my music and less time finding other work to pay the bills. Brenda finally realized this was not a hobby. She thought I was crazy, so, in 1966, we split up again. Brenda took Eddy back to Waco, and I told her I was headed off to take a shot at the big leagues: Los Angeles.

I didn't have a pot to piss in, so I went out to westbound Interstate 10 and tried to hitch a ride. I stood out there for more than an hour without getting a ride, so I finally switched to the other side of the road. The first car that came along stopped, and the guy said he was going to Memphis. I said that sounded good to me. When he let me off, he gave me ten dollars.

"What's this for?" I asked.

He said somebody did the same thing for him years ago and told him to pass it on if he ever got the chance. "Now it's your turn," he said.

My next ride was in the back of a cantaloupe truck headed east to Nashville, so I rode into Nashville smelling like a cantaloupe.

chapter four

Honky Tonk Heroes

□

Lowdown leavin' sun done did everything that needs done
Woe is me, why can't I see I'd best be leavin' well enough alone
Aw, them neon light nights, couldn't stay out of fights
They keep a-hauntin' me in memories
There's one in every crowd for crying out loud
Why was it always turnin' out to be me?
Where does it go, the Good Lord only knows
Seems like it was just the other day
I'z down at Green Gables, a-hawkin' them tables
And generally blowin' all my hard earned pay

Piany roll blues danced holes in my shoes
There weren't another other way to be
For loveable losers, no account boozers
And honky tonk heroes like me

THE TRUTH IS, I quit Nashville about as many times as I quit Brenda. I didn't know anybody there and didn't have any money, so I went back and forth to Texas all the time. I could make more money in Texas, it seemed, plus I got to see Brenda and Eddy in Waco. But I kept receiving signals that Nashville was where I was supposed to be. For example, I once fell off a scaffolding while I was carrying a bundle of shingles and fell two stories to the ground. I kept the job for six more weeks until the pain got too much and a chiropractor realized I crushed two vertebrae in my back. An old German doctor who had recently moved to the States fused the bones back together and they actually grew back stronger than before I broke them. Shortly thereafter, he died.

Still, writing songs seemed like easy work compared to that.

There are lots of famous stories about my early days in Nashville, and most of them are true.

When I first got there, I fell in pretty quick with guys that shared my primary interests: writing, drinking, and fighting. One of them was Hal Bynum, a bear of a man who also happened to be a genius. He spoke real low through his beard so you could barely understand him. But we became barroom friends, and he invited me to stay on his couch, since he knew I didn't have many other options. Hal didn't have much money either, but he fell into a pile of it a couple of years later when he wrote "Lucille," which became a monster hit for Kenny Rogers.

But, in those early days, Hal and I fell into a pattern. Each night, we would go out and get drunk. The next morning, we would wake up and eat tomatoes out of little cans. Sprinkled with salt, they were pretty tasty. Then we'd go out and start drinking again.

Even though I wasn't spending much on food, I ran out of money pretty quickly. So I got a job washing dishes, which meant I couldn't stay out as late as Hal most nights. One night, I went home early and woke several hours later to find Hal kneeling in front of the couch and holding a rusty knife to my throat. He didn't threaten me, but he kept the knife to my throat as he read aloud from Tennyson, Longfellow, and the other great poets.

I was a little shook up, but I listened. It was really great poetry and he read with such intensity. But it started to bother me when Hal started reading to me on a regular basis. Each time, he woke me with that knife to my throat. Each time, I just laid there and listened. Finally, I confided to a friend of mine what was going on.

"I can't figure out why I just lay there and take it," I said. "I guess I like the poetry."

"No," my friend said, "I think you like the knife."

It didn't take long before I figured out that Harlan Howard was the man to see about becoming a songwriter. He wrote songs for everybody, including "I Fall To Pieces," for Patsy Cline, and I knew if I could get his attention I'd be in good shape. Well, one day I screwed up my courage and drove a borrowed motorcycle over to Harlan's house. I drove straight up onto his front porch, and he came running out to see what was going on.

"Are you Harlan Howard?" I asked.

"Yes, I am."

"My name's Billy Joe Shaver, and I'm the greatest songwriter in the world."

He thought about it for a minute, then said, "Hell, I thought I was."

But he invited me inside and listened to a few of my songs while we sipped on some whiskey. He seemed to like what he heard and recommended that I go talk to Bobby Bare.

Bobby was a top recording artist. His biggest hits up to that point were "All

American Boy" and "Shame on Me." His company was called Return Music, and it was run by his father-in-law, an ex-L.A. policeman named Harlan Deck. Harlan spent most of his time at the Tally Ho Tavern—where Kris Kristofferson also was a regular—next door to the company offices. I found Harlan there one night, sidled up to his barstool, and whispered a couple of my songs into his ear. He told me to come by the office the next day and talk to Bobby.

When I got there, Bobby was sitting at his desk drinking a beer with a couple of six packs down at his feet. He was already three sheets to the wind.

"I hear you got some good songs," he said.

I told him I did.

"Good. Leave me a tape, and I'll get back to you," he said.

I told him I didn't have a tape. Well, just leave the lyric sheets, he said. I didn't have those either.

"I just got them in my head," I said.

"That's the craziest damn thing I ever heard. What if something happened to you? Nobody would ever hear those songs."

"Yeah, well, that's the way it is," I said.

Finally, he tells me to play him a song. I got about halfway through "Evergreen," and he hollered across the office, "Harlan, we got us a songwriter here."

I sat in his office and played him song after song, and Bobby got drunker and drunker. Then he said, "Let's go over to the Clubhouse."

The Clubhouse was a bar where all the top songwriters hung out, and they practically wouldn't let you inside unless you had a top ten hit. But Bobby got me in and introduced me around. Pretty soon, he was literally falling off his stool, and I had to call his wife, Jeannie, and get directions to his house so I could get him home. As soon as we got in my truck, he puked all over the dash and then passed out. I was thinking to myself, "What have I gotten myself into?"

It was freezing cold and icy that night, and I barely got my truck up the hill to Bobby's house. Jeannie came out in her robe and tried to help Bobby out of the truck. We carried him up toward the house but we lost our grip and Bobby bounced off the ice and went sliding down the hill. He was so drunk he didn't even wake up.

A couple of days later, Bobby called and asked me if I wanted a job writing songs for Return Music for fifty dollars a week. He knew I didn't have anywhere permanent to stay so he said I could sleep on the couch in the office and wash up in the sink in the back. And that's what I did.

BY 1970, four years after I came to Nashville for the first time, Bobby Bare was still paying me fifty dollars per week for writing songs. Sometimes I'd take a short-term job washing dishes or something but I tried to stay focused on songwriting. I was working plenty hard at it—I'd take a handful of amphetamines and stay up all night by myself writing lyrics on a notepad and singing them into a reel-to-reel recorder in Bobby's office. When I crashed, I'd sleep there on the couch or else out in my truck. After four years, I still didn't have a place of my own yet.

Bobby came in one morning and I was still up working on a song. It was about ten o'clock, and he pointed to the liquor store across the street where Kris Kristofferson and several of his buddies were stumbling in. "While they're out doing that stuff, you're in here writing," he said. "That's going to pay off someday."

Not long after that, Bobby introduced me to Chet Atkins, who seemed to like me, and Chet asked me to write him a tongue-in-cheek song about Vietnam. To be honest, I didn't know what tongue-in-cheek meant, so I just wrote a song based on what I thought it would be like to be in a war. I called it "Christian Soldier" and it goes, in part, like this:

> It's hard to be a Christian soldier when you tote a gun
> And it hurts to have to watch a grown man cry
> But we're playin' cards and lightin' up and ain't we having fun
> Turning on and learning how to die

When I showed it to Chet, all he said was: "I thought I said to make it tongue-in-cheek." I'm still not sure how you write a tongue-in-cheek song about war, but I guess he's right: that wasn't it.

It didn't seem like I was going anywhere, and I finally decided to head back to Texas again. I went over to Bobby's house late one night to tell him I was leaving. He tried to talk me out of it, but I was pretty down at that point, and my truck was packed and parked outside pointing south. About three in the morning the phone rang, and it was Kris and Vince Matthews. They'd been out swarming and Kris wanted to come over to talk to Bobby about his new record. Bobby convinced me to stay until Kris got there.

That was a weird time in Nashville. There were a bunch of people trying to change the image of country music, give it some class. They didn't want it to be the music of uneducated hillbillies anymore, and they hit pay dirt with Kris. He was a Rhodes Scholar and a proven songwriter—he'd recently written "Me and Bobby McGee" for Janis Joplin. Plus he made every woman in town weak in the knees. Everybody was excited because Kris wasn't out in Los Angeles writing rock 'n' roll; he was here in Nashville writing country music. I'd seen Kris at some of the bars around town, but I didn't really know him. He sure as hell didn't know me. When he got there, Bobby asked me to play Kris a song, and I picked "Christian Soldier" since it was the one I'd just finished.

When I got done, Kris said he loved that song and wanted to put it on his next album. I didn't believe him. Not only did I not believe him, but I was kind of mad about it because I thought he was actually making fun of me. That's how down I was on myself at that time. I went outside, got in my truck and drove to Texas. It wasn't until two or three weeks later that Bobby sent word to me that Kris actually put the song on his album, *The Silver Tongued Devil and I*.

Of course I turned around and headed right back to Nashville. That's where I found out that Bobby had changed the song's title to "Good Christian Soldier"—he just added the "good"—and given himself a co-credit for making a change that I didn't even want. That cost me a bunch of money over the years, but I was so glad to be on Kris's record that I didn't care at the time. Later, when Kris heard some of my other songs, he offered to produce my first album. He said he liked me because I didn't go to school, and therefore all of the thoughts that came out of my head were original. He told me most songwriters were "undetected plagiarists" whereas I was authentic. I happened to agree with him.

That was the heyday of the Opry, and the top singers were guys like George Jones, Faron Young, and Webb Pierce, and their records had what they called the "Nashville Sound." They were heavily produced, with orchestras and strings and shit you'd never find in a honky tonk. Plus, those guys had been in show business their entire lives. They didn't know anything about real life—they were just guessing at it, and it showed. I'd worked my entire life, and I knew what the hell I was talking about. I was tickled pink that somebody finally recognized that and had the guts to act on it. Kris deserves a lot of credit for that.

Kris actually borrowed money to make that album, called *Old Five and Dimers Like Me*. We finished it not long after he finished *Silver Tongued Devil*, and his record company, Monument Records, bought my record off of Kris. Looking back on it, I think they bought it just to sit on it. They knew another record company would buy it, and they didn't want it out there competing with Kris's record. Even though that record contains some of my best songs—"Old Five and Dimers Like Me," "Black Rose," and "Willie the Wandering Gypsy and Me" (not to mention my own version of "Christian Soldier")—it sat on the shelf at Monument for more than a year. Since I hadn't asked for an advance—I didn't even know there was such a thing—I didn't make a dime off that record. I was right back where I started.

Brenda had moved to Nashville when it seemed like I was about to make it, and she was not happy about the latest turn of events. Not that I could blame her. We rented a place near Lebanon outside of Nashville for fifty dollars a month, which seemed like a bargain, but it was a disaster. We heard voices at night like the place might be haunted, and when I went to the basement for the first time I found two feet of water and an enormous bee hive in the chimney. It was a stormy night, raining and lightning, and Brenda started sobbing. I grabbed my guitar and headed for the front door.

"What are you doing?" she asked. "You're going to get struck by lightning."

"I'm going to stand out there until I write at least one good song," I said.

When I came back inside a couple of hours later, I had most of "Honky Tonk Heroes." Not that it made Brenda feel much better about our situation.

Then I went to Dripping Springs and finally caught a break. Kris had invited me to head back to Texas for a bizarre music festival he was playing that summer. It was organized by Willie Nelson and a few others and included a bunch of old-timey Nashville acts like Loretta Lynn and Tex Ritter, plus some of the newer guys like Kris, Tom T. Hall, and John Prine, and even a few rock 'n' rollers like Leon Russell.

I wasn't planning to go, but Sharon Rucker, who later married Harlan Howard, insisted that I go with her, and we drove down in her station wagon. She swore it was going to be something special, and it was—more than thirty thousand people showed up in this field outside of Dripping Springs, though a good portion of them were there because of a rumor that Bob Dylan was planning to play. The crowd was a mixture of hippies and cowboys and in-betweens, and it was the first time those groups had ever really hung out together. Even though it was a financial disaster for the promoters, Willie liked the idea so much that two years later he did it again, and started calling it Willie's Fourth of July Picnic.

A couple of days before the show, I was hanging out in this trailer near the stage with a bunch of guys, drinking and pullin' on a few guitars. I didn't really know anybody but I was friendly enough, and they let me in on it. When it got to be my turn, I started playing "Willie the Wandering Gypsy and Me." I heard this commotion in the back room of the trailer, and Waylon Jennings came busting out of there, flying high on God knows what.

I was sitting there looking like some cowboy just in off the ranch in my boots, my hat, and my long hair. (I wasn't making a fashion statement with my hair. It's just that Brenda was the only one I let cut my hair, and we were split up at the time.) I knew who Waylon was, but he certainly didn't know me from Adam. He looked at me and said, "Is that your song?"

I said it was, and he asked me if I had any more cowboy songs. I said I had a whole sack of them. He said he wanted to do an entire album of those songs, and told me to come to Nashville so we could record it. (He didn't know I already lived in Nashville or that I'd already written a song for Kris—Waylon didn't pay attention to anybody but himself.) The whole conversation didn't last ten minutes, and nobody signed anything.

Well, I got pretty messed up on booze that day, and I passed out on the cement in the back of the Armadillo World Headquarters in Austin. While I was asleep, a brown recluse spider crawled up my arm and bit me on the muscle on the front of my arm. That really sent me sideways. It was like I was on acid—I was walking around like I was Jesus Christ trying to heal people for about two days. Fred Foster, who produced Roy Orbison and Kris and a bunch of other people, finally took me to the emergency room but there wasn't a lot they could do for me, even though I was supposed to play in a couple of hours. My temperature was sky-high, so I just stood in a cold shower for about an hour.

The way I remember it, I got several encores and made a big splash, but Kris says I blew my big chance to get noticed. He later wrote a song about that incident, called "The Fighter." The lyrics go like this:

> We measured the space between Waylon and Willie
> And Willie and Waylon and me
> But there wasn't nothin' like Billy Joe Shaver
> Where Billy Joe Shaver should be
> When he showed up sick later all bit by a spider
> And crazy to look in the eye
> He put on a show that was sad as it should have been
> And nobody even knew why

Despite that little mishap, I headed back to Nashville with something to look forward to. I thought the one-and-only Waylon Jennings was going to record an album of my songs. As it turned out, it wasn't quite that easy.

Waylon forgot about his promise as soon as he made it, but it was about the only thing I had going for me. I chased him around town for about six months. I'd leave messages at his office and he wouldn't call back, or I'd call and they'd say he was on the other line—I knew damn well he only had one line.

I finally caught him late one afternoon when he was recording with Chet Atkins in Studio A at RCA. The walls were lined with girls and bikers and all kinds of hangers-on. At that point, people were just waiting for Waylon to happen. He'd had a radio show when he was twelve and played with Buddy Holly. Everybody knew he was going to take off, but nobody knew when or how. Anyway, a disc jockey friend of mine named Captain Midnight got me into the studio. (Midnight was sort of famous around town because he once barricaded himself in a studio for two days when the station managers wouldn't let him play the music he wanted.) I told Midnight to tell Waylon I was waiting for him, and he came back with a hundred-dollar bill and said it was from Waylon. That just pissed me off even more—I told Midnight to tell Waylon he could stick it up his ass. Midnight wasn't about to do that, and I'm pretty sure he just stuck that hundred-dollar bill in his pocket.

I stayed there for hours knowing there was no way Waylon could dodge me—there was only one way out. He finally came out of the control room with a couple of bikers, glared at me, and said, "What the hell do you want?"

"Waylon, you said you were going to do a whole album of my songs," I said. "I've got those songs, and you're going to listen to them—or I'm going to kick your ass right here in front of God and everybody."

Everybody got real still. It was like a gunfighter moment out of a Western. Those bikers started walking toward me, ready to break me into little pieces, before Waylon stopped them at the last minute. He pulled me into a side room.

"Hoss," he said, "you just about got yourself killed."

"I've had enough of this shit," I said. "You told me something and, by God, I believed you. Where I come from, when you tell somebody you're going to do something, you do it."

Waylon was getting a little pissed off himself at this point, but he proposed a compromise. He promised to record "Willie the Wandering Gypsy and Me" and he would consider several other songs. He told me to play one song of my choice. If he liked it, I could play one more, and so on.

"If I don't like it," he said, "you get your ass up and leave."

I had my guitar with me, and I played "Ain't No God in Mexico." He said to keep playing. I played "Honky Tonk Heroes" and then "Old Five and Dimers Like Me."

At that point, he was practically jumping up and down he was so fired up. Finally, he said, "I know what I've got to do now."

For me, it was a magical night. I knew my songs had found a home. For the first time, my English teacher, Mabel Legg, was proven right. She'd told me back in school: If you'll always be honest, you'll always be different. It just took somebody like Waylon with the guts to be different along with me.

Despite his excitement, Waylon knew he was making a monumental career choice that wouldn't be very popular with a lot of powerful people. Sure enough, Chet Atkins and the execs at RCA tried to convince Waylon that the songs were too raw and they would never sell. Lucky for me, Waylon was a stubborn motherfucker. The harder they pushed him, the harder he pushed back. He ultimately decided to use ten songs from me, this unknown songwriter. (Chet Atkins insisted he put a song called "We Had It All," which had already been a top ten record, on the album as well. It's a great song—I wish I'd written it.) Waylon also chose to use his own band instead of studio musicians, the first time that had ever been done on a country record.

We went into the studio in a couple of weeks. Those sessions were tense, and we worked hard. Contrary to popular belief, there was little drinkin' and druggin'. Waylon had stuck his neck out so far he knew he couldn't afford to screw this up. I've never been easy to deal with in the studio, and I wasn't then either, even though I didn't know the first thing about recording. But I felt like Waylon kept messing up my melodies, so I'd have to play the songs for him over and over until he could get the phrasing down. Other than that, the sessions went pretty smoothly.

We finished in a couple of weeks, and Waylon came up with the idea for the cover with all of us sitting around a bar in the studio, which I thought was genius. *Honky Tonk Heroes* captured the spirit of what we were doing—a bunch of good-ol'-boys making music that was wild and crazy and free. That's me on the left, wearing a cowboy hat and smoking a cigarette. And that's Captain Midnight behind the bar.

Waylon knew he had a hit record, and he knew it was because of my songs. The day he showed me the cover, we went out to his car and he leaned over the hood toward me.

"Tell you what I'll do," he said, "I'll find a doctor to fix your hand. He can graft some skin on there and get your fingers working again. It ain't right you walking around with half a hand."

I laughed and told him not to worry about it, but that was Waylon. He was always kind to me. We had our differences, but he had a good heart. He was a real man's man, and he always told the truth. That hurt him a lot over the years—the truth always hurts the one who tells it, and God knows I know about that—but I always admired him for that.

The label execs fought about the record for several months but finally caved and put it out in May 1973. It was an immediate hit, and it's now gone platinum five times over. I don't mean to pat myself on the back, but that record really did change Nashville. Every critic who writes about that record calls it "the touchstone of the Outlaw movement," and it really was. You used to have to wear a tie everywhere, and all of a sudden clubs were letting people in with their Levis and long hair. It made it cool to be a cowboy and opened the door for all those country boys who could run just as fast as anybody else but never got the chance. Even though Willie had been moving away from the Nashville establishment for a couple of years, he didn't record his Outlaw masterpiece—*The Red-Headed Stranger*—until 1975.

Not that it made me a bunch of friends. All the established songwriters in town were mad at me because they thought I was some guy that had just come to town. But I'd been there since 1966, and I had most of these songs in my pocket when I came to town. The ironic thing is, Waylon turned out to be the kiss of death for those songs. He was perfect for them—he did them as good as they can be done. To this day, very few people have covered those songs. And they're great songs. Even Waylon got mad at me. *Rolling Stone* ran a review that said, "the real hero here is Billy Joe Shaver," and Waylon didn't like that. He told me he was never going to record another one of my songs, and he didn't.

Brenda and I were split up when I was working on *Honky Tonk Heroes*, but we got back together soon thereafter, and I got her a job working as a stylist for Johnny Cash. I guess maybe she figured I wasn't such a dumb-ass after all. I made a bunch of money with that record, of course, but not as much as I should have, since I signed a crappy publishing deal with Bobby Bare when I first came to town. Several people made millions off that record, but not me.

Of course Monument then decided to put out *Old Five and Dimers Like Me*. Shortly thereafter, the label went bankrupt. That was the first of a string of my record companies that went out of business, leaving me in the lurch. My timing was always off just a hair. I guess that's what Kris meant when he said, "If life was a television show, Billy Joe Shaver would be on at 4 a.m."

Black Rose

□

The devil made me do it the first time
(The second time I done it on my own)

FOLLOWING THE SUCCESS of *Honky Tonk Heroes*, I was hotter than a two-dollar pistol. Whenever I walked into a club with my guitar, people shoved hundred-dollar bills in my pockets. Everybody knew those songs from *Honky Tonk Heroes* were mine, and they wanted to know what I was going to do next.

Waylon noticed that the hottest guys in town at that time were all sort of outlaws, so he wanted to do a record where a bunch of us sang each other's songs. He was going to call it *Wanted: The Outlaws*. But Brenda and I were back together and we had a little money for the first time, so Brenda decided it was time we got respectable. When Waylon came over one afternoon to ask me to do the record, she put her foot down.

"No way, by God, he's not doing it," she said. "He's been an outlaw too damn long. He's going to put that stuff behind him."

I tried to argue with her but didn't get anywhere, and eventually I gave in. After all, I was sleeping with her, not Waylon. But Waylon was pissed.

They replaced me with Tompall Glaser, so the lineup for *Wanted: The Outlaws* became Waylon, Willie, Tompall, and Waylon's wife, Jessie Colter. That record became a huge best-seller—it was the first country record to go platinum, as a matter of fact. There's no doubt that if I'd made a different decision there, my whole life would have been different. But I didn't, and that was the start of what became a difficult time for me.

Although I now had a track record as a songwriter, Bobby Bare still didn't realize what he had. I played him all of my songs, and he said he never heard anything he could sell. He even accused me of holding out good songs on him, but he simply didn't know a good song when he heard one. One afternoon, I played Bobby a new song called "Ride Me Down Easy." Bobby got up in the middle of it to go take a leak, but Johnny Rodriguez was there and he liked it. Johnny decided to put it on his record. Bobby got angry when he found out about that and went to Mercury and convinced them not to put it out as a single. Bobby then recorded it himself and, sure enough, it went to number one.

I went back and forth between Nashville and Austin to play gigs, but I didn't have money like the other guys I ran with, songwriters like Tom T. Hall, Shel Silverstein, David Allan Coe, and Mickey Newbury.

I've sung on the Grand Ole Opry many times. The first was in the seventies. Porter Wagoner introduced me and went on to say that I had written songs for Willie, Kris, Tom T., Waylon, and many others, including Bob "Die-lan." I corrected him and said it was pronounced "Dillon," not "Die-lan." He snapped back at me, "Whose show is this, anyway?" The crowd thought it was funny, but Porter came back with, "Oh, yeah, and Elvis Presley. Is that all right with you, Billy Joe?" I nodded yes. The crowd really laughed then, and Porter became a great friend along with Little Jimmie Dickens, Billy Walker, Penny DeHaven, and everyone involved with the Opry. I've called that place one of my homes since then. I believe the Grand Ole Opry is the heart of the world.

Although Waylon was originally from Lubbock, he spent most of his time in Nashville and Arizona. That meant Willie and I were the top songwriters around Austin for most of the mid-1970s, which came with a lot of perks. We became friends with great men like University of Texas football coach Darrell Royal and Houston lawyer Joe Jamail, who I believe is the greatest lawyer in the world. They would fly me down to Houston for a night, and I would sit in a living room with my guitar and play my songs for senators and astronauts. It was a crazy time.

Willie and I ran around acting like fools together many nights. I remember one night we were coming home in my truck as the sun was coming up and Willie, as usual, was wearing a bandana. For some reason he was carrying an enormous opal with him, and he tied the bandana so that the opal was smack in the middle of his forehead. While we were sitting at a traffic light, a carload of kids pulled up next to us and started laughing at the two crazy cowboys in the pickup. Willie turned to them with a straight face and said, "Someday you'll be old and crazy too." That was classic Willie.

We were really close at that time, best friends. One night I had a hundred-dollar bill, and I tore it in half and gave him one of the sections. I told him, "If we ever hit bottom again, all we have to do is find each other and we'll be okay."

Even though Willie had written "Crazy" and some other great songs, he hadn't quite taken off yet. But you always got the sense that he was charmed. One night, Zeke, who was Willie's manager at the time, and Willie walked into a bar that was showing a boxing match on television. They both were dead broke. It was a lopsided match, and one fighter was beating the tar out of the other one. Some guy said, almost as a joke, "I'll take fifty dollars" on the boxer who was winning. Willie said, "I'll take that." In the next round, Willie's man knocked the other fighter out cold, and he and Zeke were back in business.

From hanging with Willie, I also got tight with the guys around him, a ragged bunch of bikers and hippies who shared most of my bad habits. We all looked out for each other. For example, I got drunk one night in Austin and decided to stop in and see Augie Meyers, who I really respected as one of the world's great keyboard players. But I was a little cantankerous because of the booze, and it occurred to me that it would be pretty funny if I rode a bike across stage while Augie was playing. As funny as it seemed to me, Augie's crew and the crowd thought it was pretty damn stupid. They chased and cussed me out the back door. One guy was so pissed off he kept coming at me in the alley behind the club. I was in no condition to fight, so I prepared myself to take a solid beating. But my opponent got a little too fancy. He tried a karate kick and slipped, hitting his head on the ground so hard it knocked him out cold.

I knew I had to get out of there, but I made another bad decision—I chose to drive. Well, I didn't get very far before I lost control of my car and drove it through a plate-glass window and into the showroom of a car dealership. The car came to rest right in the middle of all the other cars. I walked from the dealership over to Willie's pool hall and told Zeke what I'd done.

"I really messed up good this time. I don't see any way out of this one," I told him.

"There ain't nothing so bad you can't get out of it," he told me. "You just sit right here and don't move."

Zeke came back with my car about an hour later. I never heard anything more about it.

In 1975, Willie came out with *Red-Headed Stranger*. It's a great record, and it took off nationwide, mostly because of the single "Blue Eyes Crying in the Rain." Even though I didn't have a song on the album, I took a lot of pride in it because Willie told me that if it wasn't for *Honky Tonk Heroes*, he never would have had the courage to do *Red-Headed Stranger*.

After God knows how many years of struggling, Willie became an overnight star. I realized then if I didn't put some distance between myself and Willie and all my other friends, I would never do my own thing and would probably end up messing things up for them. I remembered the gift God gave me, and even though I wasn't getting many artists to record my songs, I still considered my-self a success as long as I was writing great songs. I did keep in close touch with Poodie Locke, Willie's stage manager, since we both had roots in Waco.

Joe Jamail, Coach Royal, and Willie were and still are my best friends. I still believe to this day that Joe Jamail is the greatest human being and lawyer this world will ever know. Coach Darrell Royal is the greatest coach, and Willie is the greatest entertainer. He constantly stays in the public eye, and he's still a good-ole-boy, thank God. Willie was always good to me, loaned me money, gave me anything I asked for.

I've always been a loner and a wandering gypsy type and so has Willie, so I never seemed strange to him and that held me in good stead with everyone else.

One night we had been out late, and the sun was coming up when we reached Willie's home. Paula Carline was just a baby then, but she was at the piano just beating the fire out of it and trying to sing, but she could hardly talk. It was a great time. Willie fixed some eggs and we ate, then I got in my old truck and moved on before Connie (Willie's wife at the time) got up, because I didn't know how long Willie had been gone or what Connie's mood would be. Connie was and still is the greatest lady I've ever known.

I saw a part of Willie that I was able to put into song with "Willie the Wandering Gypsy and Me." I don't think anyone will ever get as close to describing him as that song did. Willie grew up in church, just like I did, and I prayed that morning that all his successes wouldn't cause him to stray from the values he learned there. As I drove away from Willie's house that morning, I wrote a note to put in his mailbox, but I didn't leave it. I just said a prayer and went on. The note read: "No one on earth can withstand the everlasting love of the Lord Jesus Christ."

Joe Jamail was one of my father figures, whether he knew it or not. I soaked up every word he said. In 1977, Bobby Bare sold Return Music to a company called ATV for a big pile of money. Bobby came to me with a stack of papers and said, "Here, you need to sign these so you will be included in the deal."

"Shouldn't I have a lawyer look at it?" I asked.

Bobby got mad at me, saying his company had a lawyer and that should be fine. But I sent the contract off to Joe, and he realized that I could basically negotiate my own deal with ATV since I had not signed a songwriting deal with Bobby.

"Billy, don't you dare sign anything if they offer you anything less than a hundred thousand dollars for your part, plus half the publishing rights," Joe told me. I signed the contract and sent it in, and they signed it and sent it back.

But Bobby got wind of that and came barreling in one day, screaming that I was ungrateful for everything that he had done for me over the years. He came to me with another set of papers that gave him half of all my publishing royalties. He told me if I signed it I'd get ten thousand dollars, but the whole deal would fall apart if I didn't, and people in positions of power would keep me from ever making anything of myself.

I didn't sign anything, but I took the money. I don't reckon that mattered, because I received a new contract with my name signed at the bottom. My family had to do without, but we were happier than the people who had money—we had each other, and we were close. It's an awesome ability to write like a lion and completely crush someone. Forgiveness is divine and I forgive anyone who ever wronged me. I thank God I'm able to forgive, if I could just forget.

Bobby always mistook kindness for weakness. I was a big fan of his. I always respected his talent, and I still do. I learned a lot from Bobby. Mostly what not to do, but we are still friends.

I was always too trusting, still am. The music business is set up to take advantage of people like me, people with no education who trust that most people will do the right thing. But I believed then—and still do—that an artist shouldn't worry too much about business or he stops being an artist. Most people in the music business—any business, really—keep score by the balance in your bank account. I've never done that. I never worried about money that much because I knew I could always write another song. As long as no one could take that away from me, I'd be fine. But, looking back on it, I see how it hurt my family. We lived in rent houses and drove shabby cars our whole lives because I didn't always take care of business. It's amazing, though, how many millionaires there are in the music business who couldn't spell art if you gave them the "a" and the "t."

I was friendly with most of the other songwriters around town—Tom T. Hall and David Allan Coe were among my best friends, and both are amazing song-writers—but I was more of a loner than most. But I still did what I could to help out the ones I admired. When I was hot, not long after *Honky Tonk Heroes*, I got into the habit of letting Guy Clark finish my shows. He was a terrific songwriter and just hadn't quite hit yet. So I would come out for the encore, introduce Guy, and then head off into the night after I collected from the owner. My tactic back-fired on me one night. I introduced Guy, but when I went to collect my money the owner told me he couldn't pay me until after the show. I told the owner I would be back for my money the next day and left the club. Well, I'd forgotten that Townes was there that night. The next day, the owner informed me I owed him four hundred dollars. Turns out, Townes took the stage and bought rounds of drinks for the entire bar until it closed and told the owner I was picking up the tab. It was hard to stay mad at Townes, and I didn't.

There's one other factor that held me back during that time: My reputation around town was terrible. I was raising hell almost every night and starting to get deep into drugs. It wasn't like I was addicted to anything, because I never spent any money on drugs—people just gave me stuff either because they wanted to hang around me or because they thought there was a good chance I'd do something stupid. I really was a wild man, and I'm sorry for it, but I'll say this: I didn't hide it. If that's the way I chose to live my life, I didn't see a need to lie about it. But that's not the way Nashville worked. I've watched some of the most goody-goody Nashville stars lay out lines of coke as long as your arm and drink until they couldn't stand up, but they worked just as hard to keep it secret. They knew how to control their images, while I never really cared.

And it hurt me. More than once, I stood in rooms when people didn't know I was there, and I heard them say, "Billy Joe Shaver is a hell of a songwriter. Too bad he's a drunk." Or: "Billy Joe Shaver is a hell of a songwriter. Too bad he gets in fights all the time." Or: "Billy Joe Shaver is a hell of a songwriter. Too bad he's a wife-beater."

That last one always killed me, because it wasn't true. I put my hands on Brenda once, when she was seventeen and Eddy was just a baby. She was putting drops in his mouth because he was sick, but she was doing it wrong and I tried to stop her. She got mad and slapped me, and I shoved her down the hall. That's it—that's the only time I laid a hand on her. But she had a boyfriend—a fella she got involved with when I first took off for Nashville—and he used to hit her. People assumed it was me. You can't fight a charge like that.

That's when I really went crazy. I think it was the Indian in me. I figured, if they think I'm crazy, I'll show them what they want to see. I formed a band called Slim Chance and the Can't Hardly Playboys, and we might have been the wildest hillbilly band in the history of hillbilly bands. I could have made more money playing by myself, but it wasn't nearly as much fun. We got thrown out of as many dance halls as we played—fighting, drinking, you name it. One time the band filled an empty swimming pool with concrete and left the water running, just a terrible thing to do. Don't get me wrong—we could play too. Among others, we had Freddy Fletcher, who was Willie's nephew, on drums; Bee Spears, who later became a permanent member in Willie's band, on bass; and Eddy on guitar.

For a while, we had the Waddell brothers, David and Leland. Now, I'm a hick and I admit it, but the Waddells made me sound like a downright city-slicker. They were from South Carolina. David's favorite expression whenever he was impressed or excited was "Goddamn!" only it was drawn out so it was like a dirty version of Gomer Pyle's "Goooolly!" When we played the Lone Star Café in New York, Leland asked somebody what a bagel was. David said, "Oh, you know what a bagel is. It's one of them little dogs like Uncle So-and-So had with them little old legs." We fell out on the floor laughing, and David couldn't figure out why.

My booking agent at the time kept us working so hard, we almost needed the drugs to keep going. We played with everybody from the Grateful Dead to Jerry Lee Lewis, everywhere from Europe to Australia. I mean to tell you, we played San Quentin, Lincoln Center, and every place in between. When we played Lincoln Center, Linda Ronstadt was on the bill. We got a message after the show that she wanted to see us. My guitarist at the time, Danny Finley, told the messenger, "Tell Ms. Ronstadt Billy Joe Shaver has bigger fish to fry." We were cocky as hell.

The only time I got invited to play *Austin City Limits* was during this time. But they called at the last minute, and one of my band members was deep into the drugs and we couldn't find him. They never did invite me back.

Another good friend of mine I met during this time was Dickey Betts. He invited me down to his cabin in Georgia out of the blue. When I got there, he said, "The reason I invited you down here is because I didn't know you wrote all those songs on *Honky Tonk Heroes*. I thought Waylon wrote them."

I said, "Nope, they're mine," and then told him how much I liked his band, the Allman Brothers. "'Ramblin' Man' is one of my favorite songs of all time," I said.

"Hell, I wrote that one," he said. From that point on, Dickey was like a brother to me.

Dickey invited me to go out with him to Arizona one weekend. He was married to an Indian girl who could get us into a peyote ceremony, which was almost impossible to do if you were from outside the tribe. We went to a great big teepee and sat in a circle around a fire. Peyote is a cactus bud and you usually chew it, but these Indians pounded it out and put it in a liquid and we drank it.

The Indians were beating on drums when one of them noticed I was wearing a cross around my neck. They started chanting, saying, "Jesus Christ is not your Savior" over and over. I tried to leave, but the chief told me it was a religious ceremony and I couldn't leave until sun-up. They kept chanting over and over, "Jesus Christ is not your Savior."

Then a woman came in the tent and whispered in the chief's ear. Without a word to the rest of us, he grabbed a hot coal out of the fire, stuck it in between his teeth, and walked out. He came back in about ten minutes and put his hand on my shoulder.

"You can leave," he said.

I found out the next day that a baby was choking, and the chief blew the hot smoke from that coal down the baby's throat to clear it out. As far as I can gather, he figured it was a sign from Jesus, saying, "Let my man go."

Not that I was leading a pious lifestyle. When I wasn't traveling the country playing every roadhouse and honky tonk that would book me, I was hanging around more familiar bars in Austin or Nashville and making trouble. I was back and forth between Texas and Tennessee, off and on with Brenda the whole time. I was a mess. I'll tell you one story to give you an idea of what I'm talking about.

I was a pretty good pool player, and I beat this guy at pool at a bar in Austin and picked up his girlfriend in the process—a pretty humiliating two-fer for him, but I didn't think much about it. But a year or so later, I stumbled into a different bar in Austin and that same guy happened to be the bartender. I recognized the guy but didn't really put it all together. It didn't help that I was tripping on LSD. I wasn't in the bar fifteen minutes when an attractive brunette became really friendly with me at the bar. She came and sat on my lap, and we laughed and joked until all of a sudden she ducked and I got punched right in the nose. It was a sucker punch, and the girl was in on the set-up.

The guy that hit me was named Half-Breed, and he had a reputation as one of the toughest guys in town. I guess the bartender called him once he recognized me and figured he was the man to settle the score.

"Man, you want some of this?" I asked him. "I'll give it to you."

I chased him up a half-flight of stairs, and he got behind a contraption that looked like a wooden pallet with a hole cut in the center. Fortunately, I had seen several of these devices before—one of the benefits of growing up in honky tonks. It worked like a guillotine, and they would have broken my arm if I had thrown a punch, but I didn't fall for it. I chased Half-Breed back downstairs where a group of about four other guys were ready to jump in. Meanwhile, I saw out of the corner of my eye that the bartender was pointing a shotgun at my chest. "You fucked my woman," he said.

"I didn't know it," I said, trying to be as sincere as possible. "I honestly didn't know it."

I think he could tell I was sincere, because they let me walk out of there. I had a bunch of guns in my car and considered going back in there blasting, but I'm glad I didn't. Every few months, I'd get word that Half-Breed was bragging around town that he'd whupped my ass. Whenever I went looking for him, he always laid low.

I WAS NEVER GOOD AT BEING MARRIED. I'm too much of a rambler, and marriage is like being in a fenced yard. It was hard on Brenda, for sure. She left me more times than I can count. I woke one morning to find she'd taken the car and left me with our beat-up pickup that didn't run. It was a bad day. I was hungover and depressed, and it all finally got to me. I put on my favorite clothes and my best boots and decided to end it all.

I put the gun to my head, and right before I pulled the trigger, I changed my mind. I pointed the gun at the wall and emptied the clip so I wouldn't have any more ammunition, just in case I changed my mind again. Instead of killing myself, I spent the afternoon working on the truck. Once I got it running, I went into town to find a few drinks and somebody to squeeze. As usual, I found what I was looking for. As I was driving back, I started working on a song with a moral lesson in it: Sometimes it's better to go into town and get laid than blow a hole in your head.

There's nothing more fun than putting together a good song, and I had the best time writing that one. When Brenda came home a day or two later, I met her at the door wearing nothing but my guitar and my boots. "Honey, I just wrote a hit song," I told her, and I played it. The last verse goes like this:

> A honky tonk man in a honky tonk band with a honky tonk girl
> on my arm
> I may be as ugly as an old mud rail fence but I'm loaded with
> hillbilly charm
> It's my life, and no wife of mine's goin' to tell me I can't go and
> have me some fun
> So before that ol' heifer drives back in from Waco, you can bet
> your sweet ass I'll be gone

BRENDA JUST SHOOK HER HEAD. "Everyone in town is going to know that song is about me," she said. After that, she quit going to my shows. She hated that song.

Another time, in Nashville, I got suicidal and tried to call Mickey Newbury. I thought he was the one person who could help me find a way out of this deep depression I was in. But I couldn't get him on the phone, so I drove out to his house late one night, tripping on LSD. When he showed up at the door, he was carrying a gun himself. "Oh, Billy, I'm so glad you're here," he said. "I've been so down—I was about to blow a hole in my head."

So it wasn't just me. All of us were going a little nuts.

To try to save my marriage, I quit the drinking and drugs for a long while. But then an old friend from Oklahoma, David Fries, came into town, and I picked him up at the airport. Not surprisingly, we never made it home. The cops pulled us over on Broadway in the middle of Nashville. We assumed the position, but I told the officer to cuff me. He knew me and didn't understand why I wanted to be handcuffed. After he put the cuffs on, I told him I had a .22 Derringer in my boot. He thanked me, but I still didn't pass the Breathalyzer test. So he hauled me off to jail. Somehow, David passed the test.

I called Brenda from jail and told her to come get me. Whenever the cops arrested me, they would put me in jail for a few hours until I sobered up or Brenda came to get me. They never charged me with anything, which probably didn't help me get any better.

Two or three hours later, I was asleep in the corner of the jail when she came barging in swinging her purse at me. She was dressed up all in black and every eye in the jail was checking her out—she looked good.

"I'm not doing it," she hollered. "The car is in the parking lot. You can sell that and use it for bail money. I'm headed to the airport, and I'm getting the first plane back to Texas. I'm never going to see your sorry ass again."

I paused a second, then said, "I wish you'd take a train so I could write a song about it."

That actually tickled her. She let me stew for a few more hours before she came back to get me.

chapter six

Old Chunk of Coal

□

I'm gonna kneel and pray every day
Lest I should become vain along the way
I'm just an old chunk of coal now, Lord
But I'm gonna be a diamond some day

BY THE END OF THE 1970S, I was worn out. I was doing everything I shouldn't: drugs, booze, chasing women, you name it. I was headed for an early grave. My body was breaking down and I felt sick all the time. But after a long night on the town, the only thing that could make me feel better was to head right back out and do it again, and that's what I usually did.

I came home late one night and the house was quiet. Brenda and Eddy were in bed, of course, because it was about four o'clock in the morning. I entered my bedroom and walked into this bright white light—there's really no other way to describe it. A figure was sitting on the edge of my bed, and he looked at me with cold, red eyes and shook his head. I'd been taking drugs all night and day, so I figured I was hallucinating.

But he kept shaking his head at me, and his message became crystal clear: "How long? How long are you going to keep doing this?"

I didn't want to look at this figure on my bed, and I sure didn't want to hear what he had to say, so I turned and went back out to my truck. It was cloudy, with no moon, and I drove out to the cliffs above the Narrows of the Harpeth River near Kingston Springs.

I made a list in my mind of all the terrible things I'd done over the years, and I thought about the figure on my bed. I didn't know if it was an angel or a demon, but I knew it came with a message. I didn't feel like I deserved to live. There was no way I could overcome it all. But as I walked along the cliff I came upon a spot that appeared to me to be hallowed ground. I had been there before with Eddy, and we'd noticed this spot where the slaves cut a hole in the cliff to divert water onto a nearby plantation.

At the top of the cliff, up a treacherous path, I found an altar. It looked like a huge mushroom hewn by the wind and rain. It was a hundred-foot drop from the cliff. I got between the altar and the edge of the cliff, and I could have sworn I jumped, but I found myself with my back to the cliff and my arms and head draped over the altar, begging God to forgive me. I prayed for the peace that passes all understanding, and God granted me that peace. I was on holy ground and everything around me glowed like gold. I was barefooted and realized somehow my boots had been removed and were standing beside me, waiting for me to fill them with my feet.

When my boots were on, I started walking down the trail. I was humming a tune I didn't recognize. By the time I got to the truck the song was half-written: "I'm just an old chunk coal, but I'm gonna be a diamond someday."

The next day, I rented a U-Haul, loaded up the house, and pulled Eddy out of school. I moved the family back to Texas.

I WAS SAVED, and I knew I couldn't live the way I'd been living. I quit drinking, drugging, running around with other women—I even quit cussing (though I eased back into that after a while). When we got back to Houston, I found us a little rent house on the outskirts of the city, and then I stayed in bed for about the next six months. I dried out, but it wasn't easy. I didn't even know those rehab places existed, so I handled it my own way. I just prayed and prayed and waited until all the poison was out of my system. My body shook, I slept all the time, and I couldn't keep any food down.

The only thing that tasted good was diet A&W root beer. Each day, I walked down the street to a little convenience store near the house to pick up a few cans. They sold a brand of crackers that I could handle, too, and sometimes I picked up a packet of those. But that's the only thing I could eat. I lost about 60 pounds and got down to about 170.

Then one day I turned to Brenda and said, "Fix me up some eggs."

"I don't know why," she replied, "you're just going to throw them up.'

"No, I don't believe I will," I said. And I didn't. I was finally better. I started writing songs again, and playing a lot around the house with Eddy. The first song I finished was "Old Chunk of Coal." I'd had that line—"I'm just an old chunk of coal, but I'm gonna be a diamond someday"—with me since that night on the cliff, but it took me those six months to finish the song.

Eddy was about fifteen then, and he was already the best guitarist I'd ever played with. He'd always been musical, but I didn't know he knew how to play guitar until he was twelve. We were in Nashville, and I was in the living room tuning my guitar, but I always struggled with tuning. I got frustrated and left the room. Then from the next room I heard somebody wailing on the strings, perfectly in tune and moving up and down the frets. My first thought was that somebody must have come over to the house, but Eddy was sitting there by himself.

"Can you play guitar?" I asked.

"Yeah, I can play."

"Can you tune?"

"Yeah."

"Okay, from now on you're my official tuner," I said.

After that, we played together all the time. He played on most of the demos for my album "When I Get My Wings" when he was only thirteen. He was on the road with the Can't Hardly Playboys, even if it wasn't the best environment for a boy.

We once took a gig to play two weeks straight at a place called Cowboy's in Florida. This was the cocaine era, and there was so much of it floating around in Florida you wouldn't believe it if somebody told you it was illegal.

We played four hours each night at Cowboy's and then after that job ended, we had to drive all the way to New York City for a gig two days later. All of the guys in the band were doing drugs of one kind or another, but my bass player developed a heroin problem, which was the worst. He started acting a little too crazy, and he even pulled a knife on one of the other band members. I figured I would fire him when we finished the gig in New York.

Halfway between Florida and New York, I fell asleep in the back of the van. I woke up several hours later when it jerked wildly to the left. The car on our right was trying to run us off the road. Everybody was awake, and I started counting heads. Right before I could ask, "Where's Eddy?" I noticed he was behind the wheel. I didn't even know he could drive.

Not much I could do about it at that point, so I handed the bass player a beer bottle, since he was sitting in the passenger seat with a window that rolled down. I told him to wing it at the car and get that motherfucker out of our way. The bass player wound up and flung the bottle but missed the other car completely. The other band members cracked up, but I said, "You know what? You're fired."

To this day, he thinks I fired him for missing a car with a beer bottle.

But that was how Eddy got started in the business. He got a real close look at me at my worst, which I hoped would be a good example to him of all the things not to do. That was how I rationalized my behavior. When I sobered up, I was a great father. I spoiled him. If anything, I spoiled him too much, but how can you regret that?

TO EDDY, I WAS JUST A LOWLY SONGWRITER. His heroes were guitar gods like Hendrix, Duane Allman, and Billy Gibbons of ZZ Top. One time, he came up to me all puffed up and said, "You know, you're not my real daddy."

"Oh, yeah, who is?"

"Billy Gibbons," he said.

The way he played, I almost believed him. After a show one night I watched my other guitarist bash his guitar into a wall and shatter his beautiful Stratocaster into a bunch of tiny pieces. "What'd you do that for?" I asked.

"I've been playing guitar my whole life, and some kid that can barely write his name is already better than me," he said.

Dicky Betts came to visit us in Nashville before we went back to Texas. He was blown away by Eddy. They spent hours together with Dicky showing Eddy how to play slide and other little tricks of the trade. When he left, he gave Eddy Duane Allman's 335 Gibson and a 1955 Stratocaster—two of the prettiest guitars you'll ever see. Eddy kept them his whole life. Some nights, when he was a boy, I caught him sleeping in the same bed with them.

Eddy was a shy, quiet boy. Unlike me, he didn't get in that many fights or cause trouble, but he wasn't really cut out for school either. We lived in a sketchy neighborhood in Houston, and the school was full of drugs, and I was worried about him.

So once I got sober, I decided to get back out on the road to make some money. I went to the principal at Eddy's school and said, "What if I was to take my boy out of school and take him out on the road with me? Is there a law against that?"

"Tell you what," he said, "I won't say anything as long as you promise me one thing—you don't bring him back."

We had a deal. Eddy and I put together some demos, and I got a deal to record an album with Capricorn out in California. Brian Ahern, who was married to Emmylou Harris at the time, was the producer, and when I got out to California he rejected a bunch of my songs, including "Old Chunk of Coal," and forced me to put songs from a couple of other songwriters on the album. It was the only time I've ever done other people's songs, and I hated it. I never liked that album, which was called *Gypsy Boy*. It was hard for me, because I was trying to be a better person, and I wasn't sure how to respond. If it had been a year earlier, I would have punched his lights out and walked away from it. But instead I went along with it. I remember sitting in my hotel room and weeping at night.

I put together a band, including Eddy on guitar, and we toured with Willie and Emmylou to support the album. They gave us about fifteen minutes at the start of the show, but we got booted off the tour after a couple of months. Not long after that, Capricorn went out of business and I went back to Nashville to write songs for Johnny Cash.

John was a good friend, and he actually recorded "Old Chunk of Coal" before anyone else. But John Anderson heard his version and recorded his own cut, and it got released first. At the same time, I was in the process of recording another album of my own, and I used "Old Chunk of Coal" as the title track. I was going to release it as a single too.

So I was mad as hell when John Anderson beat us to the punch. Then I heard his cut and I had to admit: It was better than mine. It's a great version of the song, and, sure enough, it went straight to number one. I made some money on the songwriting royalties, but I admit I still have a bit of regret about that. It was one of my best songs, and I didn't get a chance to ride it out on my own.

Again, that was a bit of a blessing and a bit of a curse. My agents booked me in clubs as the guy who wrote "Old Chunk of Coal," but when I showed up the club owners would be pissed. They didn't want the guy that wrote it—they wanted the guy that sang it the way they heard it on the radio.

I gave John Cash about twenty-five songs and a couple of them got recorded—but no hits. John and I stayed good friends for the rest of his life. He struggled with addiction just like I did, and just like Eddy did later. One thing I'll always treasure is that John told me he sang "Old Chunk of Coal" to himself each morning when he was in rehab. If I made his recovery a little easier, that song is worth it to me. Of course, a couple of years ago, when John was sick again, he called me and wanted to send me a box of morphine patches. He kept raving about how great they were and how good they made him feel. Oh, well, a song isn't always the only cure.

THE WHOLE TIME I PLAYED WITH EDDY, people tried to tear us apart. They told Eddy he could do better than playing tiny bars with his washed-up songwriter dad. They told me Eddy was too rock 'n' roll, that he couldn't play rhythm. More than once, people told me, "You're throwing your career away by letting your son ruin your songs."

The ironic thing is that when I was first starting out, I wasn't much of a live performer. I believed the songs should speak for themselves, and I was uncomfortable putting on a show that would distract from the words I was singing. Some people criticized me and said my live shows were not as good as my songs. Then, once I joined up with Eddy, we put on a hell of a live show, and people said the opposite: The performance took away from the songs.

Through it all, Eddy and I stuck together.

Though he was quiet and soft-spoken off-stage, he was an animal when he plugged in. I called his style controlled distortion, the way he would stretch out a note almost like B. B. King but still stay in the groove. It became popular in Nashville with guys like Travis Tritt several years after Eddy started playing that way.

The first person to notice it—other than me—was Dwight Yoakam. In 1984, he invited Eddy to play lead guitar on his first tour. They went all over the country together for about two years while Dwight became a superstar. Dwight's a good man, and he was always good to Eddy. (Steve Earle also asked Eddy to tour with him, but that didn't work out because of scheduling conflicts.)

With Eddy gone, I went back to playing in clubs by myself. I made more money that way, of course, and I enjoyed it, but I looked forward to having Eddy back by my side. When the tour was over, we fell right back into it. It may have been harder for Eddy than me, seeing as how he went from riding in Lear jets to unloading the van with me.

IN ABOUT 1990, I developed a serious problem with my neck. I had a crushed vertebra and the doctors at the VA wanted to put a steel plate in. The night before the surgery, I decided to tie one on for old time's sake. I drank a little moonshine and went to dinner with a friend at Lone Star Steakhouse in Nashville. We ran into a guy named David Briggs, a piano player who was good friends with Dicky Betts. For some reason, he decided he wanted to fight me. It was just like twenty years earlier, when it seemed like there was always some punk coming to town who wanted to prove he was tougher than me. I was wearing flip flops and an old t-shirt. I didn't want to fight anybody. I just wanted to get good and drunk before the doctors cut my neck wide open. So I started to leave, but he lunged at me and stuck his thumb in my eye. I still have problems with it sometimes because of that.

I went next door to another bar and tried to cool down but he came back at me. I was standing on the bar's porch as he came up the stairs, and I nailed him with two quick shots. One of them broke his jaw. It might have been the best punch I ever landed.

When I went in for surgery the next day, the doctor said my neck was much worse than it had been. He said he was going to have to cut deeper than he previously thought, and there was a chance he could damage my vocal chords.

"What could happen? I asked.

"You could lose your voice completely, or it could just make it an octave or two lower," he said.

"That's fine. If that happens, I'll just sing the blues," I told him.

Turns out, the operation went fine.

EDDY AND I KEPT DOING OUR THING, but we couldn't find anyone interested in doing an album like the way we played live. We were more rock 'n' roll than country, but we also did a lot of my old songs that people loved.

Finally, a producer named R. S. Field told us he would record our album, and then we could go peddle it to record labels. So we cut the album and started shopping it around Nashville. Nobody wanted it.

R. S. took it to Zoo Records out in Los Angeles run by a guy named Lou Maglia. It was a straightforward rock label, but when he heard the record he said, "Those people in Nashville may not know good music, but I sure do." He started an extension of his label, called Zoo Praxis, and based it in Nashville. Zoo Praxis put out *Tramp on Your Street,* and instead of billing it as a Billy Joe Shaver record, we called ourselves simply Shaver.

Critics liked the record better than any I'd done since *Old Five and Dimers Like Me,* and we sold more copies than any album I'd ever done. Just like with *Honky Tonk Heroes* twenty years before, Nashville jumped on board after we proved our sound could be successful.

But once again we ran into problems with the record label. The folks at Zoo Praxis argued with the parent company about our next record, and the lawyers got in such a big pissing match it looked like they were going to drop us altogether. Producer Brendan O'Brien was in Lou Maglia's office one day and overheard what was going on. Brendan was the hottest producer on the planet at the time, having done albums for Stone Temple Pilots and Pearl Jam among others. He offered to do our next record for free, and Lou said okay. We played three nights at Smith's Old Bar in Atlanta, and Brendan got a great sound out of us. We called that record *Unshaven.*

People started saying it was "the second coming of Billy Joe Shaver" and all sorts of nonsense. I'd never gone anywhere.

chapter seven

The First and Last Time

□

She was a wonderful dancer
She'd glide in and out of my door
I was just one of her partners
The one who kept beggin' for more

BRENDA AND I DIDN'T BOTHER WITH ANNIVERSARIES, because neither one of us could keep track of all the times we split up and got back together. I assumed she had other relationships when we were apart, but for many years I did not know she was in a long-term affair. In fact, I asked her on several occasions, and she told me she didn't have anyone else. I found out different later.

Brenda met this guy back when I first went to Nashville in 1966. He was an ex-convict from Waco named Larry and, by all accounts, a real bad apple. He beat her on occasion, but she kept going back to him. When I wasn't with her, she was with him, and vice versa.

In the mid-1980s, I rented an apartment for Brenda in Austin. We weren't married, but I paid the rent with the understanding that I could crash there whenever I came through town. There was a terrible rainstorm one Christmas Eve when I happened to be in Austin. The streets and creeks flooded so badly that the water started coming into the house.

Brenda was in Waco with her mother for the holidays, so I put all the furniture on blocks and stashed all her records and books in places where they wouldn't get wet. She called to check on the house because the flooding was all over the news, and I told her everything was okay. When we finished talking, she forgot to hang up the phone. I could hear her and that convict laughing and joking with Brenda's mother, Mildred. It hurt that he was spending the holidays with her family, especially because I always shared a special bond with Mildred. And it hurt that Brenda lied to me. I felt like she was stringing me along just because I gave her money and paid for her apartment. It was a blue Christmas for me.

I finally caught that convict with my bare hands. I was in town sleeping at the apartment, and I heard someone come through the front door and make a commotion downstairs. I grabbed my gun. Brenda held on to me the whole way down the stairs and begged me not to shoot. I knew that it must be the convict.

Sure enough, he was passed out on the couch. It made me so mad to see him in my house I almost saw black. I cocked the gun and told Brenda I was going to kill him. He was an intruder, I thought. I was justified in shooting him. Brenda grabbed me, crying, and tried to talk me out of it. She dragged me upstairs and tried to calm me down. I went with her, planning to get her upstairs so she wouldn't see anything when I actually shot him. He must have heard us arguing. When I got downstairs, he was gone. It was a close call for him. I'm not kidding—I would have killed him.

Don't get me wrong, I was not a monk. I enjoyed my share of women over the years, but I never gave my heart to anyone else. It was all Brenda's. The only time I came close to falling for someone else was in New York, when I met a girl named Kate at O'Looney's Bar.

The night before I met her, I stayed at the Seville Hotel with the Waddells and five or six other people sprawled across the floor in our tiny little room. I woke up about six in the morning to the sounds of New York, and grabbed my little 1929 Gibson guitar and put together a song called "The Cowboy Who Started the Fight" about an old cowboy who falls in love with a New York City gal. The last three verses go like this:

> He slid back inside his old Wranglers
> And filled up his boots with his feet
> While the subways beneath New York City
> Screamed through the veins of the street
>
> Yeah, the lady gave up without question
> The trophy she'd saved all her life
> Then she curled up beside his old weatherworn hide
> When the cowboy just laid down and died
>
> Hey, hidy hee, went a whoop through the street
> As his soul slowly winged out of sight
> The lady lived on for the child to be born
> And the cowboy found heaven that night

The next night, when I met Kate, I played her that song. She went over the moon for me, and I did the same for her. Our affair lasted a few days before I had to meet the band for a show down south. I told her I would come back as soon as I could, and I did. I drove straight back to New York at the first break in my schedule. The guys at O'Looney's told me that some Hollywood folks came through a couple of nights after I left and convinced Kate she could be a star. I didn't know whether to believe that story so I hung around New York for a few days, poking my head in O'Looney's every once in a while to see if she was around. I never found her, but while I waited I wrote another song, "New York City Girl." As I packed up to leave New York, I thought, "Well, I didn't get the girl, but at least I got the song."

My friends Jim Skidmore and Don Ray helped me as much as they could when I came to New York, and I'll always be grateful to them for that.

IN 1988, a few years before *Tramp On Your Street* put us back on the map, Eddy and I were scheduled to play a show at Antone's, the famous blues club in Austin where Stevie Ray Vaughan got started. It was South by Southwest or some other festival that week and we were one of four or five bands on the bill.

On the day of the show, we were supposed to be at Antone's at eleven o'clock. But the booking agent called and told me Clifford Antone, who owned the club, decided he didn't want us to play. He only knew me as a country songwriter, and I reckon he figured I didn't have any place in a blues club. He didn't know anything about Eddy obviously.

It turns out, Robert Duvall was in town filming the mini-series *Lonesome Dove* and called Antone's that night to tell them he was coming to my show. So about ten o'clock I got a call saying that now Clifford wanted us to play, and we were due to go on stage in an hour. Amazingly, Eddy and I were able to round up the rest of the band and make it to the club just minutes before we were announced.

After we played a couple of songs, Clifford saw some of the things Eddy was doing with the guitar, and he came on stage and sat on Eddy's amp the rest of the show. He wanted an up-close view. Eddy and Clifford hit it off after the show and became close friends.

We played about forty-five minutes, and Duvall and his crew sat right in front of stage. Someone told me he'd come just to see me, so I introduced myself after we were done. We shook hands and he said, "I sure love your music. *Honky Tonk Heroes* is one of my favorite records."

"Well, thank you," I said. "Waylon sure did a good job with it."

"No, sir. You wrote it—you're the man," he said.

We didn't spend more than ten minutes together, but I left with a good feeling toward Robert, because he didn't seem to have any ego, and he went out of his way to let me know that he appreciated my songs.

I didn't hear from him for almost five years until he called in the mid-1990s and asked me to read for a part in a movie he was making called *The Apostle*. He wanted me to read for the part of Joe, a church-going good-old-boy who is good friends with the main character, played by Robert. I found out later that Waylon and a bunch of other actors and musicians read for the part, but I got it. I'm glad I didn't know Waylon was up for it, because I probably would have dropped out if I had.

I had never acted or done anything associated with movies, but Robert gave me some advice that made it easy for me: "Billy Joe, every chance you get, don't act," he said. That's the best advice I've ever gotten.

The film was mostly shot in Lafayette, Louisiana, and Bobby—as I called him once I got to know him—put me up in a fancy hotel there. I had a presidential suite with a meeting table, a sunken floor and five or six televisions. It was the nicest room I'd ever stayed in and I was there all by myself, so I called Brenda to see if she wanted to come visit.

We were divorced—again—and she was spending most of her time with that convict, or so I'd heard. But I thought she might enjoy a trip to a movie set. Besides, Johnny and June Carter Cash were there, since June was playing Bobby's mother in the film.

Brenda drove in from Austin, but when she showed up she was exhausted and stayed in bed for almost two straight days. Plus she looked bloated and overweight, even though she wouldn't eat but one meal a day. I was worried about her, and when we wrapped shooting I took her to a doctor right away.

After the first blood test, the doctors discovered she had advanced rectal cancer. They told her they would try to treat it aggressively, but they were not optimistic. That was the start of three years of hell for us. When we got home, I told her I would take care of her and asked her to marry me again. She agreed. After all those years when she couldn't count on me, she knew that I was a different man, and I was now the only one she could count on. I moved back to Waco into her house, just a few miles from the house in Bellmead where I grew up.

Brenda started chemotherapy and lost all of her hair. She was often weak and couldn't get out of bed for days at a time. I drove her down to Austin for her chemo appointments and cleaned her wounds when she couldn't do it herself. It was tough, but I loved her and she always knew that.

Did Brenda love me? I think she did. Once, after we remarried for the last time, I asked her. She just smiled back at me, such a beautiful smile. In many ways, it doesn't matter. I stayed with Brenda because I loved her, not because she may or may not have loved me. But I think she did.

I cut back on my gigs when Brenda was sick, but I was with a new label, New West, and the execs wanted us on the road as much as possible to promote our album *Victory*. In July of 1999, they booked us in a club in New York City and begged us to go, so we did.

We left Brenda with Rosie Nix, June Carter Cash's daughter and John's step-daughter. Rosie knew Brenda from when Brenda worked for her family, and she came down to help out when Brenda got sick. But everybody knew Rosie had a serious drug problem. I did my best to keep all of Brenda's medicines locked up, but Rosie managed to stay high most of the time anyway.

When I left for New York, I told Brenda not to let Rosie drive her to Austin because I didn't trust her. But on the day Brenda was scheduled to go, she couldn't find anyone to drive her, so Rosie volunteered. Sure enough, Rosie ran off the road and got the car stuck in the median of the highway. Brenda, who was supposed to be resting in the back seat with her feet up, finally got fed up and told Rosie she would drive herself. That got Rosie ticked off, and she got out and hitched a ride back to Waco.

Brenda went through her treatments in Austin and drove back to Waco. Soon after she got home, she started throwing up blood. She called me in New York, and I told her to go straight to the hospital. The Waco doctor sent her down to Austin by helicopter. Eddy and I drove straight through twenty-four hours from New York.

Brenda was in bad shape when we arrived. The doctor came to me and said, "Billy, everything is gone. All of her organs are failing. All I can do is keep her comfortable."

I knew he was telling me that she was dying. "Don't let her hurt," I told him.

She lived for several days after that. I stayed in her room and talked to her even though I wasn't sure if she could hear me. She sat up in bed one time and said, "I don't believe it." Her eyes were wide, almost rapturous, and it was like she was in awe of whatever she saw. But she didn't say anything more.

I went to her bedside and sat there for another hour. Then a nurse, an Asian woman, came by and told me, "She's gone." I was sitting there beside her and I hadn't even noticed she'd died.

chapter eight

Star in My Heart

□

Don't waste your precious thoughts on me and my tired old
    dreams
Your soul is bursting at the seams, you are finally free, to be
Even more than you could ever dream of
You'll learn to hold your head up high and you'll make your stand
You'll look the world straight in the eye, you will never blink
To think I almost held on too long to help you

You are the star in my heart
Guess you've always known
Though we are many worlds apart
I'm still your friend
And friends will always be friends forever

EDDY SHOWED UP at Brenda's funeral high on drugs. He was with Rosie, the junkie from hell, who had the audacity to get up and sing.

As hard as Brenda's death was for me, I think it was tougher on Eddy. She was only seventeen when she had him, so when he grew up they seemed more like brother and sister than mother and son. They laughed together and partied together like kids. When she was gone, Eddy just seemed lost.

Lisa Rogers, a friend of Eddy's, told me a story about being in the cemetery with Eddy not long after Brenda died. Eddy told Lisa about something that happened several days before, when Eddy was at the grave alone. He said Brenda appeared to him in a vision and said, "Everything is going to be all right."

Eddy turned to Lisa and asked, "What do you think she meant by that?'

I believe that story because I believe Brenda must have known that Eddy was in living hell. He was in pain and he was unhappy. I know, because I've been there. It is not easy to look out from that pain and find something worth living for.

I knew Eddy was using drugs long before that. He never used them in front of me, but he always confided in me. He was a grown man and he could make his own choices, but I let him know they were dangerous and he should be very careful. I told him to pray for the strength to get better. Like all addicts, he thought he knew what he was doing.

It wasn't long after Brenda died that Eddy told me he was using heroin. He said Rosie Nix got him hooked. At first, she just convinced him to try it and so he did—four times. But he told Rosie it didn't do anything for him.

"You've got to keep trying," she told him.

Before long, he got sick if he didn't have it.

I called the Cashes and told them to get her out of Waco. I told them she was an addict, and she needed some kind of help. But they denied it. They were a funny family that way. They were the kind of people that swept things like that under the rug, which they did for years, even though just about everyone in the family carried some sort of addiction. But every family deals with its problems in its own way, and Lord knows I don't want to throw stones from a glass house.

However it happened, Eddy became a full-blown addict. He stayed in Austin most of the time with his girlfriend, who was also a junkie, and I could tell he was struggling whenever I saw him. He went out to California to a rehab clinic for a while, but he didn't seem to get much better. I think there are more drugs in some of those places than there are on the streets. When he got back, he spent most of his time at a pub in South Austin with his girlfriend. Each night after closing, they locked the doors and stayed there shooting heroin and cocaine. I hate that place. I used to play there all the time, but I'll never play there again.

I told Eddy I was going to send him away to a place where he couldn't get out until he was cured, so he got married instead. He did it just so I wouldn't have the legal authority to send him away. I tried to talk to him, but we argued more often than usual when he was using. It was like talking somebody down off a ledge—how do you know the right things to say so they won't jump?

We eventually went into the studio to record The Earth Rolls On. Ray Kennedy, our producer, brought in a bunch of studio aces to Nashville to play on the record, including guys from Wilco and the E Street Band. But they would hardly let Eddy play on it, and that hurt Eddy deeply. It was our last record together—we'd already told everyone that—and they wouldn't even let him play on most of the songs. I'm sure the record company didn't trust Eddy because they knew he was using drugs, but you don't help someone get better by breaking their heart. It just destroyed Eddy when he realized they were trying to keep him off the record.

But we did put a song on the album that is the only duet we ever recorded together. It's a song we wrote together called, "Blood Is Thicker Than Water." It's not a pretty song, but it's a pretty accurate version of what we were going through at the time.

My first verse goes like this:

> You come dancing in here with the devil's daughter
> Spilling beer and doing things you hadn't oughta
> You found her walkin' the streets carryin' a sack of quarters
> Now she's stealing rings off the hands of your dying mother
> If that witch don't leave I believe I'm gonna have to help her
> Don't you know that blood, blood is thicker than water
> Blood is thicker than water

And then Eddy sings this verse:

> Can't you see I'm down to the ground, I can't get no lower
> I've seen you puking out your guts and running with sluts
> When you was married to my mother
> Now the powers that be are leading you and me like two
>   lambs to the slaughter
> I need a friend, I'm your son, and you're always gonna be my
>   father
> Don't you know that blood, blood is thicker than water

When I wrote that verse about "the devil's daughter" I was thinking of Rosie Nix. In 2003, not long after John and June died, Rosie died too. The newspapers said there was drug paraphernalia next to her body. Like Eddy, she was a sick person who needed help. God bless her soul.

Eddy wanted to get better and he was trying his best. But it's not easy.

Not long after we finished the record, Eddy and I stopped in a church called PromiseLand on 51st Street in Austin. We played together in churches a lot, and Eddy believed in Jesus just like I did. But this time we were just there to listen and pray. At the end of the sermon, Eddy and I went down to the altar to pray together. I prayed for Eddy to get better, like I always did.

The preacher approached us with the microphone while we were praying. He asked me, "What is it that means the most to you in this world?"

I told him it was Eddy.

Then he asked Eddy what it was that meant the most to him. Eddy said it was me.

The preacher asked Eddy if he would give me up to God if God asked. Eddy said he would. Then the preacher asked the same of me.

"If God asked, would you give up your only son?"

I said, "Yes, I would."

I didn't know God would literally take Eddy from me, but he did.

EDDY HAD A HANDFUL OF SONGS READY, and he was going into the studio in January. I knew he was excited, and he told me he was going to quit the drugs for good so he could be clean for his recording sessions.

The night before New Year's Eve, at about 10 PM, the Waco police showed up at my door. I was half-asleep and rushed to the door. The officer said Eddy was in the hospital. I didn't believe them—as far as I knew, Eddy was in Austin getting ready to record his album.

But Eddy actually was in Waco. He came to town with his wife for a party to celebrate his new album, and they ended up in a dingy motel with a bunch of people doing drugs. A couple of my band members were there as well, I found out later.

When I got to the hospital, Eddy was breathing on a machine but he didn't look normal to me. A nurse told me his jaw was broken and his ribs were kicked in, which I didn't understand. I stood over him and told him I loved him, and I prayed for him. It seemed like he was trying to come back, like maybe he was trying to move his lips, but I wasn't sure. Before long, the nurse said they needed to take him upstairs to see if he was brain-dead. When she came back, she said that he was. Eddy was dead.

By then, it was New Year's Eve.

I don't know exactly what happened. One story I got is that Eddy passed out from the drugs but everyone was so scared of getting arrested that they called the drug dealer instead of 9-1-1. When the drug dealer showed up, he shot Eddy full of something that killed him. But that doesn't explain why he was beat up so bad.

Nothing made sense to me. Two hours before, I'd been sleeping in my bed, and now I had lost the one person who meant more to me than anything else in the world. At that moment, I was mad at everybody. I went outside to make sure his wife was all right. I didn't want her anywhere near Eddy. When I tried to go back inside, the police wouldn't let me back in the hospital. I explained to them that my son was in there, but they didn't budge, and eventually they threatened to arrest me if I didn't leave peacefully.

In the next few days, I requested police reports from the incident and an autopsy of the body. I called over and over, trying to get some answers. The police called it an accidental death, but I don't accept that. Eventually, the sheriff's department called and told me I needed to leave it alone—apparently, Eddy's father-in-law was a big-shot police officer from New York, and someone told me he pulled some strings to keep things under wraps. Finally, I let it go. The Bible says, "Vengeance is mine, sayeth the Lord." I turned it over to Him. But I will say this: That drug dealer is dead, and it was not by my hand.

What do I believe in my heart? Eddy struggled with drugs, I know that, but I think he was murdered that night. I don't know if the drug dealer did it or someone else who might have had a life insurance policy on him. But I don't think Eddy died from the drugs alone. If it was just the drugs, why were his ribs smashed and his jaw broken? Why would they not allow me to have an autopsy?

The morning after he died, I woke up in my house alone. Eddy had been living in Austin since Brenda died, so I was used to being in the house by myself, but I felt so alone that morning. Eddy and I were scheduled to play that night at Poodie's Hilltop, a bar outside of Austin owned by Willie's road manager. I decided I was going to play the show for two reasons: one, because Eddy always insisted we never miss a gig; and, two, because if I had stayed at home alone that day, I'm not sure what I would have done to myself.

Willie put together a band and we played for a couple of hours. I joined in on a few songs, but Willie and the other guys played the majority of the songs. Most of the audience didn't know about Eddy's death yet, and it was New Year's Eve so people were just partying and having a good time. But occasionally I saw someone start to cry and leave the bar. That's when I knew word was starting to get out.

After the show, I stayed with Willie at his home. We stayed up late into the night talking. He lost a son, Billy, who was a dear friend of mine, so Willie knew a little of what I was going through. More than anything, Willie tried to convince me not to take revenge on the drug dealers. Willie and I have a lot of water under the bridge together, just like any two friends who have known each other for thirty-five years. But he stepped up for me during that time, and I truly appreciate it.

A few days later, Willie, Freddy Fletcher, and some others called to say they were going to pay for the funeral expenses. I was in bad shape financially at the time, and they knew I couldn't pay for the kind of funeral Eddy deserved.

I offered to pay them back later but they wouldn't accept anything. The only thing I could give were Eddy's guitars, the ones that belonged to Duane Allman. Willie kept them at his recording studio for many years, and so I just never asked for them back. I heard there was a fire there not long ago. I don't know if the guitars made it.

chapter nine

Try and Try Again

□

Well I went up on the mountain
And I looked down on my life
I had squandered all my money
Lost my son and wife
My heart was filled with sorrow
And I almost took my life
But I found the strength inside me
To give life one more try

SOON AFTER BRENDA AND EDDY DIED, one of my best friends, Kinky Friedman, booked a bunch of shows, and he and I and what was left of his band, the Texas Jewboys, played to sold-out crowds across Texas. For that, I will be eternally grateful—to Kinky and the people who showed up to watch us play.

With Brenda and Eddy gone, there wasn't much for me to do in Waco. So I stayed on the road. My friend, Jessie "Guitar" Taylor, helped me put a band together. We played wherever they would book us, even though it damn near killed me. First, I had another three disks removed from my neck and a plate put in their place. The doctors told me to wait six weeks before I started driving again, but I was back on the road in three.

In August of 2001, I played at Gruene Hall, the oldest dance hall in Texas and one of its best. But if you've ever been to Central Texas in August, you know it's hotter than blue blazes. It was about 101 degrees outside and 130 degrees on stage under the lights. Not long after we started, I felt chest pains, though that's not really the right word for it. It was more like a herd of elephants were stomping on my chest. There was no mistaking it—I was having a heart attack. I distinctly remember thinking, "Thank you, Jesus, for letting me die on the stage of this honky tonk. It's where I belong. I'm going to join Brenda and Eddy."

The pain got worse and worse, but I didn't die. Because I'd had some heart trouble before, I carried nitroglycerine with me. Unfortunately, I washed it in my clothes the night before, and the nitro was just a bunch of crumbs in my pockets. I shoveled it into my mouth but I don't think it was really at full strength after going through the washer and dryer.

We eventually played more than three hours. Jessie is deaf in one ear, and I kept telling him that I only wanted to play one more song. He thought I was saying, "let's do one more" so he would launch right into another song as soon we finished the last one.

We had a gig in Pflugerville the next night, and I drove to a motel there for the night. At this point, I was pissed. Instead of dying at Gruene Hall, one of the all-time great dance halls, I was going to be found dead in a motel in Pflugerville, of all places. Not quite as romantic. But it rained cats and dogs the next day, and the club canceled the show. I headed home to Waco.

When I finally got to the doctor, he found that only one of my arteries was functional and its blood flow was only ten percent of what it should have been. They immediately put stents in my arteries to increase the blood flow, and told me I needed to schedule a quadruple bypass.

When my old friend Kinky Friedman heard about my planned surgery, he wasn't too pleased. See, we had already booked a month-long tour of Australia. "People have heart attacks every day," Kinky told me. "You're going to ruin my career if we cancel this tour."

Of course, I should not have listened to Kinky—it's never a good idea to listen to Kinky, actually—but I did. We played to big crowds over there, but I just barely made it through. I was grouchy and tired the whole time, which is not a good combination around Kinky, who likes to stick the needle in a little bit. I finally had to tell him, "Kinky, you've got to cut it out or I'm going to knock the shit out of you."

But although I think Kinky was half-way serious about fearing I would ruin his career, I also think he had my best interests at heart. He figured I needed to be anywhere other than sitting at home alone.

One afternoon, on a long highway between gigs, we heard over the radio that Waylon died. We pulled over to the side of the road and uncorked a bottle of wine. It seemed strange to be in the middle of Australia toasting Waylon, but there we were. It was a sad day. Waylon was a truth-teller and one of the greatest singers of all time. I miss him.

Two days after I made it home, Dr. Chip Oswalt in Austin performed my quadruple bypass. He is one of the best, if not the best, surgeons in the world and I was lucky to have him. Marsha Milam, a good friend of mine in Austin, introduced me to Dr. Counts, who was a close friend of Dr. Oswalt's, and he agreed to do the operation. Not only that, I was lucky to have health insurance—see, I joined the Screen Actors Guild when I worked on *The Apostle,* and the insurance paid for my operation. It took an hour and forty-three minutes, and Dr. Oswalt, who was a longtime fan, told me later that he actually listened to one of my CDs while he operated.

A LOT OF PEOPLE want to know what my life is like today.

Well, I read the Bible every day. See, after Brenda died, I took responsibility for her two pit bulls. They say if you read the Bible out loud, it will scare away the bad spirits. Let me tell you, my dogs, they got some bad spirits in them. So sometimes I read out loud.

But, more importantly, I read the Bible to stay close to Jesus. He is the most important thing in my life. I've had people ask me whether I think Brenda and Eddy died for my sins, like their deaths were some sort of karmic penalty for my past mistakes. Nope, no way. Jesus died for my sins. End of story.

I don't blame Jesus for what has happened to me. Just the opposite: He gives me the strength to carry on each day.

It makes some people uncomfortable that I talk about Jesus all the time. They want me to stick with songs about drinking and honky tonks and cowboys and freedom. I play those songs, because they are a part of my life and I'm proud of them. Hell, I still write them. But I also play songs about Jesus.

People say I should keep my religion to myself. But I'm not talking about religion. When you accept Jesus Christ as your personal savior, he is your personal savior—not somebody else's. I believe you should worship the God of your choosing, but it's all just a different way of describing Jesus. You know how some people say you can't be all things to all people—well, Jesus can. We don't know how he does it. It's beyond our comprehension. Whatever you need to do to get the job done and be close to Jesus is the right way to do it. Don't let some knucklehead tell you that because you don't speak in tongues, you can't go to heaven. Or because you don't go to church every Sunday, you can't go to heaven.

I go to church sometimes. My uncle, Bill Honea, is a preacher and sometimes I'll go listen to him. Or sometimes I'll go to a little one-room church in Gholson, outside of Waco. It's a holy rollers' church where you can jump up and down and no one will look at you funny. Some Sundays, I stay home and watch football. But I read the Bible every day. It's how I stay close to Jesus and you know what I say? If you don't love Jesus, go to hell.

I still live in Brenda's house in Waco that I took over after she died. I don't do much—I just write songs. Sometimes I'll go hang out with my friend Jimmy

Hollingsworth. He's a mechanic and his son, Jerry, is a guitarist in my latest band.

But I stay on the road most of the time. It's where I feel most at home. That hasn't changed since I was a kid. Besides, most of the time it keeps me from dwelling on Brenda and Eddy. But not all the time.

Eddy always believed he was lucky when the clock turned to 1:11 or 11:11. Sometimes, when I'm on the road, I'll request Room 111. But sometimes when I forget, I get that room anyway. And a lot of times, when I'm on stage, I'll feel his presence.

On a recent night on the road, I sat back in bed, a pillow beneath my head, knowing I needed to sleep but unable to get the sounds from the couple in the next room out of my mind. The way the woman was moaning, I could just see her face and the way she moved her body as she and the man went at each other like tigers. Even though it had been four years since the death of my one and only love, I couldn't help but drift back to those days when Brenda and I first made love in a beat-up shack on the banks of the Bosque River. It was glorious. It was gut-wrenching. It was maddening. And it stayed that way for almost forty years.

The sounds from the next room kept me awake the entire night, thinking of Brenda. When we were right, there was nobody better. It was almost like we were perfect. I loved her with all my heart and soul but deep down, I now believe, she felt something different. She loved being loved by someone who completely loved her. She searched and searched but I was the only one who could give her the love—physical, spiritual, and mental—that she craved.

The next morning, I dressed early to see the couple as they left the room. In particular, I wanted to see the woman, to see how she compared to Brenda. But they never left, and when I walked past the room I saw that the beds were made and the room was empty. The clerk at the desk told me no one stayed there that night.

That is the way my life is since Brenda and Eddy passed. Their ghosts surround me, appearing at strange and wonderful times. I don't want to die—most days, anyway—but I look forward to the wonderful day when I will be together with Brenda and Eddy again.

IN 2002, I released a record called *Freedom's Child*. It contained a song called "Day by Day" that tells the story of my life with Brenda and Eddy. It's one of my favorite songs, but I've never performed it live, and I don't think I ever will.

The album spent eight weeks at the top of the Americana charts and got good reviews from the critics. To tell the truth, I've always gotten good reviews.

The critics kept me alive over the years. It seems like they appreciated my music more than the industry as a whole, which never seemed to know what to make of someone like me.

In many ways, the last couple of years have been very rewarding for me. My good friend Robert Duvall produced a documentary about me, and it was directed by his girlfriend, the beautiful and talented Luciana Pedraza. I don't know what is going to happen with that, but Bobby says he wants to nominate it for an Academy Award. I don't know about that, but I've enjoyed working closely with Bobby and Luciana and it's an honor that they think I'm worthy of a film like that.

Maybe I should have known my luck was due to change. While we were shooting the documentary, Luciana's crew followed me to a honky tonk where my friend Dale Watson was playing and they were hosting a chicken shit contest. They marked squares at the bottom of a hen's cage and dumped a bunch of feed in there with the hen. Whoever owned the square where the hen took a shit got the prize.

I had a feeling about that hen. It was a dominecker hen just like I wrote about in my song "Black Rose," and I talked to that hen and told her right where to do her business. Sure enough, she dropped it right on my square.

My luck's been pretty good ever since. I'm reasonably healthy, and it seems like people are paying more attention to my music than ever before. After Johnny Cash passed, I learned that he had written that I was his favorite songwriter. And Willie Nelson told a couple of magazines that I was the best songwriter alive today. Kris Kristofferson told Mario Tarradell of the Dallas Morning News: "He's as real a writer as Hemingway." Those kinds of compliments mean a lot to me.

It seems like everyone has something nice to say about me these days. It's funny, though, because sometimes it reminds me of the old boxer, Earnie Shavers. He fought all comers for many years but none of the top heavyweights wanted to step in the ring with him. He knocked out more than fifty fighters before he finally got a shot at the title. But he was too old by then. He was no longer a threat, and he lost. God bless him.

But I'm not done yet. I'm still writing songs, and I'll be on the road as long as I can drive and as long as I can see the microphone.

Most songwriters, it seems to me, write as a means to an end. The song is an attempt to create a single. Or it's an attempt to get a cut on Tim McGraw's latest record.

To me, the song is poetry. That's all it is. It's the way I describe the world around me, make sense of it. When I lost my fingers, Jesus made it clear to me that writing songs is my mission in life. I've stayed true to that ever since, and

I always will. I believe my songs will live long after I'm gone. I hope you like them. I sure do.

People sometimes ask me, "Who is your favorite songwriter?" Sometimes I answer, though it changes from day to day. Kris Kristofferson is always near the top of the list, but I also love Willie, Rodney Crowell, Leonard Cohen, Bob Dylan, Paul Simon, David Allan Coe, Tom. T. Hall, Mickey Newbury, Dicky Betts, and Todd Snider. There's so many of them. As I live longer, this list will grow until every writer in the world is on it.

But the more I think about it, I think the best songwriter is the one who makes you feel like you are in the best place in the world when you are listening to his or her songs. The one who makes you understand yourself a little better when your ears hear their words. At that moment, that songwriter is the best. That's the beauty of the song.

Lyrics

Complete Lyrics to the
Recorded Songs Written by Billy Joe Shaver

□

☐

BLACK ROSE
THE DEVIL MADE ME DO IT THE FIRST TIME
(THE SECOND TIME I DONE IT ON MY OWN)
BY BILLY JOE SHAVER

Way down in Louisiana
Amongst the tall grown sugar cane
Lived a simple man and a dominecker hen
And a rose of a different name

The first time I felt lightnin'
I was standin' in the drizzlin' rain
With a tremblin' hand and a bottle of gin
And a rose of a different name

The Devil made me do it the first time
The second time I done it on my own
Lord put a handle on this simple headed man
Help me leave that black rose alone

When the Devil made that woman
Lord he threw the pattern away
'Cause she were built for speed with the tools you need
To make a new fool every day

Way down deep and dirty
On the darkest side of shame
You'll find this cane cuttin' man doin' it again
With that rose of a different name

The Devil made me do it the first time
The second time I done it on my own
Lord put a handle on this simple headed man
Help me leave that black rose alone

OLD FIVE AND DIMERS LIKE ME

BY BILLY JOE SHAVER

I've spent a lifetime making up my mind to be
More than the measure of what I thought others could see
Good luck and fast bucks are too few and too far between
There's Cadillac buyers and old five and dimers like me

She stood beside me letting me know she would be
Something to lean on if everything ran out on me
Fenced yards ain't hold cards and like as not never will be
Reasons for rhymers and old five and dimers like me

It's taken me so long now that I know I believe
All that I do or say is all I ever will be
Too much ain't enough for old five and dimers like me
Too far too high and too deep ain't too much to see

L.A. TURNAROUND

BY BILLY JOE SHAVER

Stuck here in Los Angeles with a case of worn out souls
Totin' a bag full of yesterdays and a mind full of doughnut holes
I been talkin' 'bout leavin', but I just can't go
Los Angeles hang-ups won't turn a-loose of my soul

Cold Los Angeles women far as I can see
Losin' time a-makin' time with a country boy like me
I wanna go where that wind blows with a southern drawl, y'all
L.A. turn around, turn loose of my soul

L.A. turn your big eyes out to sea
L.A. turn around, don't look at me
Let me go home where I belong
Where the nights are short as the days are long
Where they're too busy livin' to think about dyin'
L.A. turnaround, turn loose of my mind

Sweet sweet sweet Virginia, turnin' around in my mind
Used to be all over me, now you're somewhere behind
If I ever get back South, gonna shut my mouth
And try to turn my wrong side inside right side out

L.A. turn your big eyes out to sea
L.A. turn around, don't look at me
Let me go home where I belong
Where the nights are short as the days are long
Where they're too busy livin' to think about dyin'
L.A. turnaround, turn loose of my mind

GEORGIA ON A FAST TRAIN

BY BILLY JOE SHAVER

On a rainy Wednesday morning, that's the day that I was born
In that old sharecropper's one room country shack
They say my mammy left me the same day that she had me
Said she hit the road and never once looked back

Now I just thought I'd mention my grandma's old age pension
Is the reason why I'm standing here today
I got all my country learning milking and a churnin'
Picking cotton, raisin' hell, and bailing hay

I been to Georgia on a fast train honey
I wuddn't born no yesterday
I got a good Christian raisin' and an eighth grade education
Ain't no need in y'all treatin' me this way

Now sweet Carolina, I don't guess I'll ever find another
Woman put together like you are
I love your wiggle in your walkin' and your big city talkin'
And your brand new shiny Plymouth rag top car

Well it's hurry up and wait in this world of give and take
Seems like haste it makes for waste every time
I declare to my soul when you hear those ages roll
You better know I'm gonna get my share of mine

I been to Georgia on a fast train honey
I wuddn't born no yesterday
I got a good Christian raisin' and a eighth grade education
Ain't no need in y'all treatin' me this way

WILLIE THE WANDERING GYPSY AND ME
BY BILLY JOE SHAVER

Three fingers whiskey pleasures the drinker
Moving does more than the drinking for me
Willie he tells me that doers and thinkers
Say movin's the closest thing to being free

He's rosined his riggin', laid back his wages
He's dead set on ridin' the big rodeo
My woman's tight with an overdue baby
And Willie keeps yelling hey Gypsy let's go

Willie you're wild as a Texas blue norther
Ready rolled from the same makin's as me
And I reckon we'll ramble till Hell freezes over
Willie the wandering Gypsy and me

Now ladies we surely will take of your favors
And we'll surely warn you there never will be
A single soul livin' can put brand or handle
On Willie the wandering Gypsy or me

They dance on the mountains, they shout in the canyons
They swarm in a loose herd like wild buffalo
Jammin' our heads full of figures and angles
And tellin' us shit that we already know

Willie you're wild as Texas blue norther
Ready rolled from the same makin's as me
And I reckon we'll ramble till Hell freezes over
Willie the wandering Gypsy and me

LOW DOWN FREEDOM

BY BILLY JOE SHAVER

Long haired young girl here beside me
Fit my body, warmed my mind
Sleepin' quiet, never knowin'
By tomorrow she'll be one more thing I'm gonna leave behind

Like them big wheels I'll be rollin'
Like them rivers gonna flow to sea
Cause I'd rather leave here knowin'
That I made a fool of love before it made a fool of me

First Chorus:
Lowdown freedom you done cost me
Everything I'll ever lose
You're as empty as my pockets
From the top of where you start down to the bottom of my boots

Open highway lonesome wind moan
Tell me somethin' I don't know
Wrap them woman arms around me
Tell me why I'm gonna leave when I don't really wanna go

Lowdown freedom you done cost me
Everything I'll ever lose
You're as empty as my pockets
From the top of where you start down to the bottom of my boots

Second Chorus:
Lowdown freedom you done cost me
Everything I'll ever lose
You're as empty as my pockets
And you're colder than the water that keeps soakin' through my
    boots

JESUS WAS OUR SAVIOR AND COTTON WAS OUR KING
BY BILLY JOE SHAVER

The wagons was a-rollin' with a cobble colored sound
When me and little David rode our first load into town
The cotton gin was a-ginnin' out the pennies for the pound
Like a giant vacuum cleaner suckin' lint up off the ground

Our freckled faces sparkled then like diamonds in the rough
With smiles that smelled of snaggle teeth and good ol' Garrett snuff
If I could I would be tradin' all this fatback for the lean
When Jesus was our Savior and cotton was our king

This kind of life we're livin' beats all I ever seen
Guess some of us was born for pickin' things and eatin' beans
Still I reckon we're all diggin' something well within our means
Cause Jesus is our Savior now, but cotton ain't our king

Our freckled faces sparkled then like diamonds in the rough
With smiles that smelled of snaggle teeth and good ol' Garrett snuff
If I could I would be tradin' all this fatback for the lean
When Jesus was our Savior and cotton was our king

SERIOUS SOULS

BY BILLY JOE SHAVER

Cool was the stream flowin' clear from the mountain
To the grassy green valley below
Yes, and many were the days we all drank from that fountain
Leavin' no way but downhill to go

First Chorus:
We're all wayfarin' wanderin' gypsies alone
Looks like lookin' for is where we'll always be
Cursed to be born as serious souls
No one will take seriously

Lord, I've touched me the country, I've seen me the light
I've found what I wanted to find
And of ready-rolled livin' and takin' and givin'
I've had more than my share of mine

Second Chorus:
We're all wayfarin' wanderin' gypsies alone
Looks like lookin' for is where we'll always be
Cursed to be born as serious souls
No one will take seriously

BOTTOM DOLLAR

BY BILLY JOE SHAVER AND DANNY FINLEY (ALIAS PANAMA RED)

Bottom dollar it looks like the end
Oh how I hate to see you go
Bottom dollar we've been the best of friends
We must have counted on each other a hundred times or more

Oh and my oh my how those eagles fly
Goodbye bottom dollar goodbye

Bottom dollar all your friends have gone
They've been blown on dance hall gals and wine
Bottom dollar if the truth was known
You've been the bestest friend I'll ever find

Oh and my oh my how those eagles they do fly now
Goodbye bottom dollar goodbye
Goodbye bottom dollar, goodbye old friend of mine

TEXAS UPHERE TENNESSEE
BY BILLY JOE SHAVER

I come up here from Waco on a U-Haul-it freight
In my mind Tennessee to me was just another state
Now I weren't tryin' to get into I's just swingin' on your gate
But I'm about to go down under from this hurry up and wait

First Chorus:
So won't you roll me another one, don't try to mother me
I know I can't see the forest but I think I feel the trees
And anyway goin's where I guess I'm always gonna be
I declare I feel like Texas when I'm uphere Tennessee

I done built myself a highway on your ceiling in the hall
Over yonder in the corner gettin' turned on by the wall
Come the morning that old dawning will be breakin' up like me
Ain't no holler log what I can't hog when I get up a tree

Second Chorus:
So won't you roll me another one, don't try to mother me
I know I can't see the forest but I think I feel the trees
And anyway goin's where I guess I'm always gonna be
I declare I feel like Texas when I'm uphere Tennessee

THE GOOD LORD KNOWS I TRIED

BY BILLY JOE SHAVER

From the very first hello until the very last goodbye
From here to there and everything between
All I ever did was try my best to keep you satisfied
And all you ever did was make a fool of me

I tried every way I knew to give you everything I had
And all I ever did was try to treat you right
Still the best that I could do was never good enough for you
I couldn't please you but the good Lord knows I tried

My old friends they tried to warn me but I paid them all no mind
When I see them now we don't have much to say
For you took everything we had and left me nothing but behind
Feelin' like some old forgotten yesterday

I tried every way I knew to give you everything I had
And all I ever did was try to treat you right
Still the best that I could do was never good enough for you
I couldn't please you but the good Lord knows I tried

WHEN I GET MY WINGS
BY BILLY JOE SHAVER

Been a whole lot of people thought me a fool
Been a time or two I thought that I was one too
Ain't a chain that can hold me, ain't a thing I won't try
When I get through livin' I'm gonna die

Gonna die with my boots on, gonna go out in style
With a free-wheelin' feelin' and a honky tonk smile
And if the Devil don't dodge me, gonna spit in his eye
When I get my wings I'm gonna fly

Gonna fly away singing I'm gonna fly
Gonna wrap my new wings 'round
A few feathered things in that free feelin' sky
Gonna reach a new heaven, higher than high
When I get my wings
Hey I'm gonna fly
Gonna fly away singin'
Fly away singin'

AIN'T NO GOD IN MEXICO
BY BILLY JOE SHAVER

Down the road a-ways I've heard say a new day's comin' on
Where the women folks is friendly
and the law leaves you alone
I'll believe it when I see it and
I haven't seen it yet
Don't mind me keep on a-talkin'
I'm just lookin' for my hat

First Chorus:
Ain't no God in Mexico
Ain't no way to understand
How that border crossin' feelin'
Makes a fool out of a man
If I'd never felt the sunshine
I would not curse the rain
If my feet could fit a railroad track
I guess I'd a been a train

Me and Weezie Higginbotham used to chase across the yard
Back in 1947 that's when more than times was hard
Pity me I didn't find the line in time and like a fool
In front of God and everybody I politely blew my cool

Ain't no God in Mexico, ain't no comfort in the can
When you're down 'round Matamoros gettin' busted by the Man
If I'd never felt the sunshine
I would not curse the rain
If my feet could fit a railroad track
I guess I'd a-been a train

LOVE YOU 'TIL THE COWS COME HOME
BY BILLY JOE SHAVER

Got a roundhouse right, got a straight razor in my shoe
Got a roundhouse right, got a straight razor in my shoe
Got a pocket full of money, honey, ain't nothin' I can't do

Come on over here, Momma, gonna love you 'til the cows come
    home
Come on over here, Momma, gonna love you 'til the cows come
    home
Till the cotton are picked and the hay is in the barn

My woman she fat to the heart and the right kind too
My woman she fat to the heart and the right kind too
I know she love to do the things we do

Slide on over here Momma, gonna love you 'til the cows come home
Get on over here honey, gonna love you 'til the cows come home
Till the cotton are picked and the hay is in the barn

Play that down-home music like it's never been played before
Play that bad-ass guitar like it's never been played before
When you get through pickin', let me hear it all over some more

WOMAN IS THE WONDER OF THE WORLD

BY BILLY JOE SHAVER

Recitation:
Lord in love let there be conjugal felicity
Let the mother of another one be born
So the whole world can see throughout eternity
Woman is the Mother of us all

Man has been to the moon, done 'bout all a man can do
But a woman is the wonder of the world
From her head to her toe man ain't thought what she don't know
Yes, a woman is the wonder of the world

Woman is the wonder of the world
She may be high society or just a good old-fashioned girl
When she was made she put a shade on Mother Nature's pearl
She ain't much, she's just the wonder of the world

Woman is the wonder of the world
She may be high society or just a good old-fashioned girl
When she was made she put a shade on Mother Nature's pearl
Yes a woman is the wonder of the world

WHEN THE WORD WAS THUNDERBIRD
BY BILLY JOE SHAVER

Up every morning at the crack of dawn
Nights are short as the days are long
Life turned out to be another magazine

I'm livin' with a stranger now
The girl I knew got away somehow
She went out with two-bit gasoline
I wanta go back, you know what I mean

Yeah when the word was Thunderbird
And the price was forty twice
Drinkin' wine and lovin' you was fun
Ah, but love turned out to be a passin' thing
A different bird of a different wing
And some damn fool put a dollar twenty nine
On a jug of Thunderbird wine
And Lord I don't know if I'm gonna make it
Don't know if I'll have the strength to take it
Everything's hung up in yesterday

Married to a civic-minded social girl
Takin' short cuts in a woman's world
She won't let her hair down when I'm home
Society is just slavery
And security is a-killing me
I worked hard for it but I'd give it all away
If I could go back to yesterday

Yeah when the word was Thunderbird
And the price was forty twice
Drinkin' wine and lovin' you was fun

AMERICA YOU ARE MY WOMAN
BY BILLY JOE SHAVER

By your way, I've often traveled
Magic mother of the pearl
Watched your mysteries unravel
While each foamy wave uncurled
'Neath my soul the sands of freedom
Fertile valleys, mountains high
Blistered by the blazing sunshine
Mellowed by the moonlit night

First Chorus:
Mighty measure of the maker with your welcome arms unfurled
America, you are my woman
America, you are my world

Many worlds in dreams I've traveled
Sliding softly thru the night
Scanned through silicones and cycles
Mirrored low your emerald light
When my days on earth return to
Dust from whence my body weighs
Will my soul could always tarry
Where the same's first flight was made

Second Chorus:
Mighty measure of the maker with your welcome arms unfurled
America, you are my woman
America, you are my world

A RESTLESS WIND

BY BILLY JOE SHAVER

A stone thrown from Heaven skippin' 'cross the water
With disappearing ripples left behind
A book with no cover, a rhyme with no reason
Guess I'll always be one of the roving kind

Cause moving's in my soul, I guess a gypsy got a-hold
Of somebody in my family long ago
And if some night while half asleep you hear the back door softly
    squeak
You'll touch my empty pillow, then you'll know

   First Chorus:
That a restless wind is calling me again
Her warming hand is tuggin' at my soul
Summer's gone, winter's comin' on
And I can't let it catch me standin' in the cold

Life made dice out of my bones and it won't leave me alone
'Til it warms me up and takes another roll
You can't roll seven every time, so there ain't no use in cryin'
It don't take an educated head to know

That when I'm movin' down the road I won't need no overload
Nor memories of you to weigh my mind
And every step I wait will be one more I could take
That would put those memories further down the line

   Second Chorus:
And a restless wind is calling me again
Her warming hand is tuggin' at my soul
Summer's gone, winter's comin' on
And I can't let it catch me standin' in the cold

EVERGREEN

BY BILLY JOE SHAVER

An old man sat on the evergreen and this is the song he sang

Thru evergreen fields of my youth I'd go singing
My steps left no footprints behind
No fruit of the harvest lent weight to my pockets
Small knowledge was stored in my mind

Now youth has forsaken this old man
My seasons are numbered by three
No seeds have been sown in the plowed fields
No harvest is waiting for me

A cripple for life is the fate of a loner
No fruit will be borne by his tree
These thoughts pierce my mind while in echoes of memory
A small voice too late calls to me

Come run through my green fields you old man
Search beyond your windowsill
Go touch my high mountains and valleys
Come sleep 'neath my evergreen fields

WE STAYED TOO LONG AT THE FAIR

BY BILLY JOE SHAVER, BOBBY BARE, AND CHARLIE WILLIAMS

We've stayed too long, much too long at the fair
The sweet cotton candy smell of love has left the air
They're tearing down the happy rides and they'll move them God
    knows where
We're standing here alone and the laughter is all gone
I think we've stayed too long at the fair

Only fools and little children refuse to realize
That a fairground's painted lanterns are just lights in your eyes
The Ferris wheels and roller coaster rides all have to end
And everybody has to come back to earth again

We thought that big calliope would never end its song
But we should have known a merry-go-round can only turn so long
I guess we just weren't ready for the carnival to end
So we stood there frightened and alone when the real world set in

HONKY TONK HEROES

BY BILLY JOE SHAVER

Lowdown leavin' sun done did everything that needs done
Woe is me, why can't I see I'd best be leavin' well enough alone
Aw, them neon light nights, couldn't stay out of fights
They keep a-hauntin' me in memories
There's one in every crowd for crying out loud
Why was it always turnin' out to be me?
Where does it go, the Good Lord only knows
Seems like it was just the other day
I'z down at Green Gables, a-hawkin' them tables
And generally blowin' all my hard earned pay

Piany roll blues danced holes in my shoes
There weren't another other way to be
For loveable losers, no account boozers
And honky tonk heroes like me

CHICKEN ON THE GROUND
BY BILLY JOE SHAVER

There's an old familiar hillside overlooking Emhouse, Texas
Where I left some childhood memories layin' 'round
I can almost hear the singing, I can still remember praying
At them old campground meetings eatin' chicken on the ground

With them hallelujahs ringin', everybody shoutin', singin'
Give me that old-time religion, Jesus loves me, this I know
When life was finger-lickin' good and God lived in our neighborhood
At them old campground meetin's eatin' chicken on the ground

I can still remember feelin' all that happiness inside me
When I praised the Lord and laid my burdens down
But that chicken must have tasted better than the word of God
'Cause it went slippin' through my fingers and rollin' on the ground

With them hallelujahs ringin', everybody shoutin', singin'
Give me that old time religion, Jesus loves me, this I know
When life was finger-lickin' good and God lived in our neighborhood
At them old campground meetin's eatin' chicken on the ground

I reckon everyone of us can call back or remember
When the taste and smell of youth was all around
And I reckon in our own way everyone of us is payin' now
For eatin' chicken and not listenin' to old Parson Brown

With them hallelujahs ringin', everybody shoutin', singin'
Give me that old time religion, Jesus loves me, this I know
When life was finger-lickin' good and God lived in our neighborhood
At them old campground meetin's eatin' chicken on the ground

SLOW ROLLIN' LOW

BY BILLY JOE SHAVER

I got a slow rollin' low
My doin's damn near undone me
Done got me so down and bent out of round
Don't know my head from my toes

Ain't a hand here to hold
Ain't a shoulder to cry on
Ain't a lesson to learn nor a corner to turn
Twixt the dyin' and me

Lord, I wanted to be
Something you could depend on
Lawdy, Lawd, woe is me
Ain't a body would care

I got a slow rollin' low
Forgot the words to my song
Ain't that just like a fool to want a ride on them trains
When the trains is all gone

SILVER WINGS OF TIME
BY BILLY JOE SHAVER

The evening sun is sinking, moving homeward
As darkened shadows claim the fight they won
With upturned eyes closed from the light of darkness
And two crossed hands that raised another's son

Gone, oh gone the one who really loved me
For what I was not what I ought to be
Who never questioned falling leaves in autumn
Nor silver nests built on a dying tree

In gingham gown she warmed me from the coldness
The winter nights seemed warm as summertime
Another love will never touch as deeply
As love that flew on silver wings of time

On pension for the aged she raised a young man
Who learned the love of God and other things
Now, love he knew that twelve times warmed his winter
Has flown away on time's bright silver wings

YOU ASKED ME TO

BY BILLY JOE SHAVER AND WAYLON JENNINGS

Long ago and far away
In my old common labor shoes
I turned the world all which-a-ways a
Just because you asked me to

Like unto no other feel
Simple love is simple true
There's no end to what I'd do
Just because you asked me to

Let the world call me a fool
But if things are right with me and you
That's all that matters and I'll do
Anything you ask me to

Knowing how much I love you
And after all that we've been through
I'd turn and walk away from you
Just because you asked me to

Let the world call me a fool
But if things are right with me and you
That's all that matters and I'll do
Anything you ask me to

FIT TO KILL AND GOING OUT IN STYLE
BY BILLY JOE SHAVER

Got a Stetson and some brand new blue jeans
Got a wad of bills that'd choke a whooping crane
I come from Waco, Texas, and I've been around this world
I tell you boys I'm hittin' high and wide

Got a pickup truck you know what I mean
Got a whatchacall like you ain't never seen
I'm a pistol-packin' poppa with a million dollar smile
I'm fit to kill and goin' out in style

Fit to kill and goin' out in style
Fit to kill and goin' out in style
I'm still a little crazy and I'm still a little wild
I'm fit to kill and goin' out in style

My woman is the queen of the world
Yea, she ain't just an ordinary girl
She makes country lovin' like an oyster makes a pearl
I'm gonna let her hold my heart a while

We're the talk of the town every night
We do our thing until the morning light
We're a head above the highbrows by a money-makin' mile
We're fit to kill and goin' out in style

Fit to kill and goin' out in style
Fit to kill and goin' out in style
We're still a little crazy and we're still a little wild
We're fit to kill and goin' out in style
Fit to kill and goin' out in style

NEW TEXAS WALTZ
BY BILLY JOE SHAVER

New Texas waltz my friend
We are sweethearts again
Here where it all began
Dancing the new Texas waltz

You are the one I have waited to hold
You are more precious than diamonds or gold
Now is the time all my dreams will come true
Dancing the new Texas waltz with you

New Texas waltz my friend
We are sweethearts again
Here where it all began
Dancing the new Texas waltz

Way over there in that star-studded sky
Acres of memories go twinkling by
Love that was dead has come back alive
With you and the new Texas waltz tonight

New Texas waltz my friend
We are sweethearts again
Here where it all began
Dancing the new Texas waltz

SATURDAY NIGHT

BY BILLY JOE SHAVER

It's Saturday night
I said Saturday night
Feelin' so durn right
Yeah it's Saturday night

I got my paycheck cashed
Broke out my best stash
Gonna tie one on, dance all night long
Lord, it's Saturday night

It's Saturday night
I said Saturday night
Feelin' so durn right
Lord, it's Saturday night

Gonna hit the spot
Where the music's hot
You know them kick-ass songs really turn me on
Lord it's Saturday night

It's Saturday night
I said Saturday night
Feelin' so durn right
Lord it's Saturday night

Gonna find me a girl
Gonna give her a whirl
Gonna lay it on the line, have a big old time
Lord, it's Saturday night

It's Saturday night
I said Saturday night
Feelin' so durn right
Yeah it's Saturday night

RAGGED OLD TRUCK

BY BILLY JOE SHAVER

Early this mornin' without any warning I took me a look at myself
   (good God)
I seen how this married-up life I'd been livin' was tryin' to choke me
   to death
I laid on the bed with my gun to my head and I nearly 'bout ended it
   all
But I come to myself just before I got killed, and I blowed me some
   holes in the wall

I'm thinkin' bout crankin' my ragged old truck up and haulin' myself
   into town
I'm thinkin' bout raisin' so doggone much hell I'll die 'fore I live it all
   down
I've laid 'round this place 'til I'm blue in the face and I may as well be
   underground
I'm thinkin' bout crankin' my ragged old truck up and haulin' myself
   into town

A honky tonk man in a honky tonk band with a honky tonk girl on my
   arm
I may be as ugly as an old mud rail fence but I'm loaded with hillbilly
   charm
It's my life, and no wife of mine's goin' to tell me I can't go and have
   me some fun
So before that ol' heifer drives back in from Waco, you can bet your
   sweet ass I'll be gone (long gone)

I'm thinkin' bout crankin' my ragged old truck up and haulin' myself
   into town
I'm thinkin' bout raisin' so doggone much hell I'll die 'fore I live it all
   down
I've laid round this place till I'm blue in the face and I may as well be
   underground
I'm thinkin' bout crankin' my ragged old truck up and haulin' myself
   into town

I'M JUST AN OLD CHUNK OF COAL

BY BILLY JOE SHAVER

I'm just an old chunk of coal
But I'm gonna be a diamond some day
I'm gonna grow and glow till I'm so pluperfect
Gonna put a smile on everybody's face

I'm gonna kneel and pray everday
Lest I should become vain along the way
I'm just an old chunk of coal now, Lord
But I'm gonna be a diamond some day

I'm gonna learn the right words to talk
Gonna search and find a better way to walk
I'm gonna spit and polish my old rough-edged self
'Til I get rid of every single flaw

I'm gonna be the world's best friend
Gonna go round shakin' everybody's hand
I'm just an old chunk of coal now, Lord
But I'm gonna be a diamond some day

I'm gonna be the cotton pickin' rage of the age
I'm gonna be a diamond some day

(WE ARE) THE COWBOYS
BY BILLY JOE SHAVER

The Texans are gathered up in Colorado
The kid with the fast gun ain't with 'em today
The cowboys are ridin' tall in the saddle
They shoot from the heart with the songs that they play

There's a right handsome woman on up around Boulder
Got slick hardwood floors and a potbellied stove
She swears I am someone she can believe in
She's the best Colorado gal I ever knowed

We are the cowboys, the true sons of freedom
We are the men who will get the job done
We're pickin' our words so we don't have to eat 'em
We're roundin' 'em up and a-drivin' 'em home

The cowboys are average American people
All of 'em's different just like me and you
They love this old world and they don't want to lose it
They're countin' on me and they're countin' on you

The world will breathe easy when we stop the bleedin'
The fighting will end when all hunger is gone
There's those who are blind so we'll all have to lead 'em
It's everyone's job 'til we get the work done

We are the cowboys, the true sons of freedom
We are the men who will get the job done
We're pickin' our words so we don't have to eat 'em
We're roundin' 'em up and a-drivin' 'em home

MEXICO
BY BILLY JOE SHAVER

There's a place I am goin' a way over yonder
Far from the bustling crowd
Where the coyotes howl in the soft silver moonlight
Oh God, I wish I was there now

In Mexico where the wild cactus grow
And the guitars so leisurely play
Where the wrinkled old men in their dusty serapes
All sleep 'til the middle of day

The brave Rio Grande caresses her body
And graceful it glides crossed her land
She always will be my sweet señorita
And I'll always be her man

So come hell or high water I'm leavin' tomorrow
Nothing' can stop me this time
By seven days travel I'll be back in the saddle
Down south of that old borderline

In Mexico where the wild cactus grow
And the guitars so leisurely play
Where the wrinkled old men in their dusty serapes
All sleep 'til the middle of day

IT AIN'T NOTHING NEW BABE

BY BILLY JOE SHAVER

Well it ain't nothing new babe
It's just a dream that fell through babe
And the plans that you have to make
Will be made here and now with your head slightly bowed

You can see life goes on girl
And the weak must grow strong girl
On your journey through this old world
You will soon understand that the love of your man

Was a shoulder to cry on
And a friend to rely on
But it wasn't worth dyin' for when he told you goodbye
When he told you goodbye

Now there's one thing for certain
The pain won't stop hurtin' till you go back to workin'
With something left that you love
'Cause the push and the shove

Of the everyday day now
Has become such a hassle
And your only dream castle disappeared in the sky
When I told you goodbye

Well it ain't nothing new babe
It's just a dream that fell through baby
And the steps that you have to take
Will be taken somehow, they'll be taken right now

THE ROAD

BY BILLY JOE SHAVER

The road it never changes but the people always do
Sometimes I'm half a mind to tell 'em so
The path along the riverside is sparkled now with dew
Stretching here to where God only knows

I will always love you girl, on that you can rely
There's nothing more or less you'll need to know
So lay your pretty head back in the crook of my old arm
And love me one more time before I go

Along some lonesome highway I'll be thinkin' back on you
I'll let your warm love shield me from the cold
A melody in memory so shiny bright and new
Reelin' with the rhythm of the road

Early in the morning just before the sun comes up
You'll miss me makin' noises round the stove
You'll touch the empty place where my warm body use to lay
And curse the day I left you for the road

AMTRAK (AND AIN'T COMING BACK)

BY BILLY JOE SHAVER

She's Amtrak and ain't comin' back
She's Amtrak and ain't comin' back
She took everything she wanted in an old gunny sack
She's Amtrak and ain't comin' back

My baby wears them spike-heeled boots
My honey wears them high-heeled boots
She wears them black leather boots
Lord, she tied me up and turned me loose
She's leaving on that new rail train

She's Amtrak and ain't comin' back
She's Amtrak and ain't comin' back
She took everything she wanted in an old gunny sack
She's Amtrak and ain't comin' back

She use to be my hot hippie honey
Yes and I was her natural man
Then all of our troubles got started
When I joined up with this hillbilly band

I started staying out all hours of the night
And winding up drunk and in jail
The last thing she said through them cold iron bars
Was this time I won't go your bail

She's Amtrak and ain't comin' back, Lordy Lord
She's Amtrak and ain't comin' back
I guess she might have stayed if I'd cut her some slack
She's Amtrak and ain't comin' back

She's Amtrak and ain't comin' back, Lordy Lord
She's Amtrak and ain't comin' back
I guess she might have stayed if I'd cut her some slack
She's Amtrak and ain't comin' back, Adios honey

HOW MANY HEARTS MUST YOU BREAK

BY BILLY JOE SHAVER

I've known you such a long long time
And your wife is a good friend of mine
God knows she's got every right to do wrong
But she's not the trifling kind

She would lay down her life for you
That's more than the others will do
But I wonder how long she can keep hangin' on
To someone who's proven untrue

How many hearts must you break
Just look at the chances you take
The fool in your arms may be your last mistake
How many hearts must you break

I once heard a wise man say
These lessons worth learning today
The stars only come out when night time rolls 'round
And idols have feet made of clay

You see I can see me in you
And I know what you're coming to
The tables you selfishly set for yourself
Will soon be turning on you

How many hearts must you break
Just look at the chances you take
The fool in your arms may be your last mistake
How many hearts must you break

OKLAHOMA WIND
BY BILLY JOE SHAVER

Jesse lit us up and passed the bottle one more time
We used to smoke and drink a lot back then
Thunder shook the heavens and the lightning danced the sky
Like I ain't seen since can't remember when

The Oklahoma Kid lay dyin' in a women's wing
Just another Indian bitin' dust
Clouds grew dark and promised but they didn't rain a thing
The government ain't something you can trust

We picked a gig in Tulsa at the Cain's Ballroom that night
The Oklahoma Kid was dead and gone
Rain still hadn't come but the clouds still blacked the sky
That's when I took the time to write this song about the wrong

Oh the Oklahoma wind slides crost the burning sand
Over double crosses Mother Nature made
And nothin's ever come as far as I'm concerned
From those dead tomorrows planted yesterday

Black man took a chance and got his foot hung in the door
He sure as hell is gonna have his day
Red man speaks his peace to gain his long-lost dignity
And Washington just turns the other way

Jesse spends his days in Loco Hills, New Mexico
Every night he drinks his fill of booze
When Ruidoso's running he lays his money down
Winnin' just enough to lose and lose and lose and lose

Oh the Oklahoma wind slides crost the burning sand
Over double crosses Mother Nature made
And nothin's ever come as far as I'm concerned
From those dead tomorrows planted yesterday

TELL ME VIRGINIA
BY BILLY JOE SHAVER

Tell me Virginia what would you do
If the cover was torn from the book about you
Would you wear them tight dresses and the symbolic hose
That a woman like you would call her working clothes

Tell me Virginia
What would you do
If everyone knew
What I know about you

Say there Virginia self-made Robin Hood
Girl you give it to the poor man but you ain't no good
'Cause you married that rich man and dragged yourself down
When you went for that fast buck on the dark side of town

Tell me Virginia
What would you do
If everyone knew
What I know about you

Hello Virginia won't you burn that red fire
Girl to light up your bedroom and show what you are
Them straight shoes you're wearin' would not cramp your feet
If you stayed in that big house and off'n the street

Tell me Virginia
What would you do
If everyone knew
What I know about you

Tell me Virginia
What would you do
If everyone knew
What I know about you darlin'

ONE MOVING PART

BY BILLY JOE SHAVER

Too tall talking puts me walkin'
Don't let it get up next to me
Signifyin' and downright lyin'
Don't hang around me long enough to be
See I learnt real young down on the farm
Simplicity don't need to be greased
I got it all down to one moving part
And that moving part is me

Footloose free and easy me
Ain't up to nothing but having fun
Ain't too many women left that I ain't loved on
Ain't too many crazy things that I ain't done
I'm-a on my own country born, I come and go and do as I please
I got it all down to one moving part
And that moving part is me

Yah I got it all down to one moving part
And that moving part is me

SWEET MAMA

BY BILLY JOE SHAVER

Sweet mama, lay your burdens down
Sweet mama, lay them trophies down girl
Come here and I'll tell you 'bout some truth in life I've found
Sweet mama, set yourself right down

You know pride it ain't worth a U.S. dime
No pride it ain't worth this poor man's time
It's misery to be so jealous all the time
Sweet mama, be kind to your mind

Sweet mama, girl now you're sure feelin' fine
You may think this is just a line
I only put these words into this little song
To try girl and help us get along

HARDWORKIN' MAN
BY BILLY JOE SHAVER

I am a hardworkin' man
Just doin' the best that I can
I'm easy to please and I'll do in a squeeze
Yeah, I am a hardworkin' man

My hands is both callused and worn
There's some fingers that's gone offa one
I'm rough as a cob, but I do a good job
Yeah, I am a hardworkin' man

Hardworkin' man yes I am
I'm a hardworkin' man
I'm the salt of the earth all across this great land
Yes, I am a hardworkin' man

On the day that I lay down and die
There ain't too many folks gonna cry
But I bet you my boots, I won't be wearin' no suit
When I say my last good goodbye

Hardworkin' man, hallelujah
I'm a hardworkin' man
I'm the salt of the earth all across this great land
Yes I am a hardworkin' man

MANUAL LABOR
BY BILLY JOE SHAVER

From the Garden of Eden right on up through today
By the sweat of his brow is how a man's supposed to earn his pay
But the VIPs and the rich folks of this land
Think manual labor ain't nothin' but a Mexican who crossed the Rio
    Grande

Manual labor, that old backbreaker, he
Sure knows how to make a fool out of folks like me
He throws your muscles in a hustle and he numbs your brain
Then he hauls you off down the tracks like a runaway train

Oh manual labor, you old backbreaker, you
I must have mistaken you
For a true-blue friend
You've never been
My youth and my good times spent
Don't know where my money went
I allow how the government
Got more than their share
Oh well, who cares
I'm a-getting' on a holy roll
Sent a dollar to the TV show
God knows how the money grows
When you're saving a soul
Big save on souls

HILL COUNTRY LOVE SONG
BY BILLY JOE SHAVER

When the mornin' sun comes peepin' o'er the mountain
And nature's melody begins to play
I wonder how a song that seems to be so short and sweet
Could be as good again another day

Oh, I loved you with a passion hot as summer
And I picked you when you were as fresh as spring
I held you when the autumn wind blew in the winter cold
And warmed you 'til the meadow turned to green

Now the evenin' sun is sinkin', movin' homeward
As I bid another peaceful day goodbye
Our home is on the south side of an old Hill Country town
Nestled here beneath the Texas sky

And when you touch my hand I know that you still love me
And I know you know I'll always feel the same
'Til every season's day has come and gone and come and gone
And come and gone and come and gone again

YOU JUST CAN'T BEAT JESUS CHRIST

BY BILLY JOE SHAVER

He was born to be known as everybody's brother
He is the Father's son and Mary is His mother
He is a 'scuse my slanguage, well a compound country kinda guy
Ain't no way to get around it, you just can't beat Jesus Christ

I used to crank and drink until my back was to the floor
I'd take it to the limit, then I'd try to get some more
Yes, when it came to gamblin', well Lord God knows I'd roll them
    dice
Ain't no two ways about it, I have been saved by Jesus Christ

Even though I am a sinner He will always be my friend
Well He starts in the middle and He does not have an end
And when my soul was held for ransom, yea He is the one who paid
    the price
Ain't no reason to deny it, I owe it all to Jesus Christ

FUN WHILE IT LASTED

BY BILLY JOE SHAVER

I met her one evening in a barroom downtown
She was the picture of truth
Her shoulders were sagged and her head was bowed down
Like me, she was livin' the blues

When the music had ended and the crowd dwindled down
And we were the last lonely two
We left with each other when nothing was left
And nothing left better to do

And it was fun while it lasted, but it didn't last long
Before we knew it the thrill was all gone
And we both wound up singin' the same lonesome song
It was fun while it lasted, but it didn't last long

I had a woman and she had a man
Before we both lost it all
When I thought of her that's when she thought of him
And I never could stand that tall
And it was fun while it lasted, but it didn't last long
Before the mornin' I'd picked up and gone
And we said goodbye singin' the same worn-out song
It was fun while it lasted, but it didn't last long

WHITEMAN'S WATERMELON
BY BILLY JOE SHAVER

From Maine to California I learned to live the blues
When I was just a young man I learned to sing the blues
When I holed up in Memphis I learned to write 'em too

Yeah the white man's watermelon sellin' all the time
Yeah the white man's watermelon sellin' all the time
I make my livin' writin' watermelon rhymes

Yeah the poor old southern white trash they sure can sing the blues
Yeah the great American public Lord they sure can pick and choose
The Allman Brothers Band can rock you plumb out of your shoes

Yeah I sold some songs in Macon, sold some in L.A. too
Yeah I sold some songs in Nashville, sold some in Austin too
Unless I miss my guess, folks, I'm sellin' some to you

Yeah the white man's watermelon sellin' all the time
Yeah the white man's watermelon sellin' all the time
I make my livin' writin' watermelon rhymes

STREET WALKIN' WOMAN

BY BILLY JOE SHAVER

Low down low, roll on roll
Lower than the bottom ever is
Graveyard cash it can't outlast
The money makin' monkey shakin' kid
She high hot and easy boys
Low rent mama all right
She got no damned use for too-tall blues
She got a better reason not to cry

She bought them holes in the sole of her shoes
One-way winner ain't about to lose
Yeah the woman,
The old street walkin' woman

Oh mama lion, why your kind
You wanna treat a lady like a whore
You strut your stuff away so much
You never get enough of wantin' more
You lie like the Devil, girl
You shake your fist at the man
You got wrong on right, screwed up so tight
That you don't even have to give a damn

You shape to break every man you make
And swear it's all for goodness sake
Make me want some, whoa
Some old street walkin' woman
Walk on, woman
Swing that purse and shake that ass

GOOD NEWS BLUES
BY BILLY JOE SHAVER

My woman left me and I'm sure glad she did
My old gal left me and I'm glad she took the kid
Now I got less mouths to feed
And more room to sleep in the bed

I got the good news blues, smilin' on a rainy day
Got the good news blues, done sung all my troubles away
Ain't got no achin' bones
Ain't got no bills to pay

The politician he say what you want to hear
Lord it's hear one day and right out the other ear
He'll promise you whiskey and
Won't even give you a beer

Got the good news blues, smilin' on a rainy day
Got the good news blues, done sung all my troubles away
Ain't got no achin' bones
Ain't got no bills to pay

HEART OF TEXAS

BY BILLY JOE SHAVER

The heart of Texas where I was born
I'm proud to say the Lone Star state's where I'm comin' from
God almighty's been good to me

Where I grew up learnin' bout the Alamo
With a swelling pride down deep inside me
Sayin' "go man go," you can be all you want to be

Yeah, it's right there where the best is
Smack dab in the heart of Texas
Thank you ma'am

Papa run off before I was born
Mama picked cotton just to raise us kids in the Texas sun
We grew up in the cotton fields

So I learned how to work and I learned how to fight
I learned how to put a bunch of words together as the years rolled by
God gave me a way to go

When my sweetheart listened to the songs I played
She said "I love you honey, but there ain't much money in a serenade
I need a man with a real job"

Now she's back there where I left her
God knows I still think about her now and then
But she knows these clothes I'm wearin'
Is the kind that shirttail's always flappin' in the wind

I made my music from coast to coast
Been over the water, couldn't get much hotter, then I damn near
    froze
Remember the Alamo

The road was long but the heart is strong
I was Texas born and raised and Texas is still home
Texas is home sweet home

Yeah, it's right there where the best is
Smack dab in the heart of Texas, thank you ma'am
Where my songs are always playin'
And them good old Texas gals say "Honey, where ya been?"

LIVE FOREVER
BY BILLY JOE SHAVER AND EDDY SHAVER

I'm gonna live forever
I'm gonna cross that river
I'm gonna catch tomorrow now
You're gonna wanna hold me
Just like I've always told you
You're gonna miss me when I'm gone

Nobody here will ever find me
But I will always be around
Just like the songs I leave behind me
I'm gonna live forever now

You Fathers and you Mothers
Be good to one another
Please try to raise your children right
Don't let the darkness take 'em
Don't make 'em feel forsaken
Just lead 'em safely to the light

When this old world is blown asunder
And all the stars fall from the sky
Remember someone really loves you
We'll live forever you and I

I'm gonna live forever
I'm gonna cross that river
I'm gonna catch tomorrow now

I'm gonna live forever
I'm gonna cross that river
I'm gonna catch tomorrow now

I'm gonna live forever
I'm gonna cross that river
I'm gonna catch tomorrow now

IF I GIVE MY SOUL
BY BILLY JOE SHAVER

Down a dangerous road, I have come to where I'm standin'
With a heavy heart, and my hat clutched in hand
Such a foolish fool, God ain't known no greater sinner
I have come in search of Jesus, hopin' He will understand

I had a woman once, she was kind and she was gentle
Had a child by me who grew up to be a man
Had a steady job, 'til I started in to drinkin'
Then I started playin' music, travelin' with the Devil's band

Oh the years rolled by like a mighty rush of eagles
Our dreams and plans were all scattered to the wind
It's a lonesome life when you lose the ones you live for
If I make my peace with Jesus, will they take me back again

If I give my soul, will He clean these clothes I'm wearin'
If I give my soul, will He put new boots on my feet
If I bow my head and beg God for His forgiveness
Will He breathe new breath within me and give back my dignity

If I give my soul, will He stop my hands from shakin'
If I give my soul, will my son love me again
If I give my soul and she knows I really mean it
If I give my soul to Jesus, will she take me back again

TRAMP ON YOUR STREET
BY BILLY JOE SHAVER

A long time ago, no shoes on my feet
I walked ten miles of train track to hear Hank Williams sing
His body was worn but his spirit was free
And he sang every song looking right straight at me

I'm just a tramp on your street
You must understand
You got my soul at your feet
And my heart in your hand

Now I don't have to pick and I don't have to choose
I don't have to win and I don't have to lose
If I make any pay I just throw it away
I don't count on tomorrow, I just live for today

I'm just a tramp on your street
You must understand
You got my soul at your feet
And my heart in your hand

Still you opened yourself
And you held me inside
You made a stray dog like me
Feel welcome tonight

We're just tramps on your street
You must understand
You got our souls at your feet
And our hearts in your hand

Still you opened yourself
And you held us inside
You made stray dogs like us
Feel welcome tonight

I'm just a tramp on your street

THE HOTTEST THING IN TOWN
BY BILLY JOE SHAVER

She's the queen of the red hot mommas, the hottest thing around
When she shows up at a honky tonk she can righteously get down,
You know she'll get on down, plum down to the ground
She's the cat's meow and the dog's bow wow
The hottest thing in town

A friend of a friend of a friend of mine said he knew her well
Said she hung around heaven 'til she learned too much
Then she headed straight for hell
She went straight to hell, everything for sale
She walks the walk and talks the talk
The hottest thing in town

She's the hottest thing in town by a country mile
She can lick her lips and roll her hips
And really drive you wild
She's got everybody's number, she's making all the rounds
She's a hell of a heavenly ball of fire
The hottest thing in town

Someday I'll get lucky and slide into her town
And maybe if she digs me we'll go round and round and round
Go round and round, burn the whole town down
We'll be the red hot dame and her latest flame
The hottest thing in town

She's the hottest thing in town by a country mile
She can lick her lips and roll her hips
And really drive you wild
She's got everybody's number, she's making all the rounds
She's a hell of a heavenly ball of fire
The hottest thing in town

WHEN THE FALLEN ANGELS FLY
BY BILLY JOE SHAVER

I have climbed so many mountains just to reach the other side
And I've near drowned myself in freedom just to feed my foolish pride
On my journey through the darkness I have finally seen the light
I know no one's ever loved me like you're loving me tonight

There is something you must tell me, you think I won't understand
How you found such worldly pleasure in the arms of other men
I would never try to judge you, we have both been wrong and right
But I know no one's ever loved you like I'm loving you tonight

God will save His fallen angels and their broken wings He'll mend
When He draws their hearts together and they learn to love again
All their sins will be forgiven in the twinkle of an eye
All the saints rejoice in Heaven when the fallen angels fly

There's a story in the Bible about the eagle growing old
How it grows new sets of feathers then becomes both young and
    strong
Then it spreads its mighty wingspan out across the open sky
We will have the wings of eagles when the fallen angels fly

When the fallen angels fly
When the fallen angels fly
We will have the wings of eagles
When the fallen angels fly

TAKE A CHANCE ON ROMANCE
BY BILLY JOE SHAVER

Oh the music such sweet perfume
Drifting across the room
A beautiful melody
When you were in love with me
Now the tables have turned again
Here we are, we are the best of friends
Come on honey dance with me
Let me hold you again

Take a chance on romance baby
Don't you know I'm still in love with you
It wasn't so long ago
I recall how you loved me too
Come on while the music plays
Don't you turn around and run away
Come on honey dance with me
Take a chance on romance

Such a wonderful remedy
Has been given to you and me
We can fall back in love again
Take a chance on romance

Take a chance on romance baby
Don't you know I'm still in love with you
It wasn't so long ago
I recall how you loved me too
Come on while the music plays
Don't you turn around and run away
Come on honey dance with me
Take a chance on romance

Take a chance on romance baby
Don't you know I'm still in love with you
It wasn't so long ago
I recall how you loved me too
Come on while the music plays
Don't you turn around and run away
Come on honey dance with me
Take a chance on romance

I WANT SOME MORE

BY BILLY JOE SHAVER

Every day I face the lonesome morning
I try and get my feet back on the floor
I can't recall the reason why you left me
But I still feel the slamming of the door

Like a child whose mama left him cryin'
Like a miser who cannot hold his gold
I ain't been worth a nickel since you left me
I can't get enough of you, I want some more

I want some more of what it is you gave me
I wanna feel the way I felt before
I tried and tried but I just can't forget you
I can't get enough of you, I want some more

You came to me the same way that you left me
You played your game and evened up the score
It's best to leave the party when it's happening
Or stop the show and leave 'em wanting more

I want some more of what it is you gave me
I wanna feel the way I felt before
I tried and tried but I just can't forget you
I can't get enough of you, I want some more

HONEY BEE

BY BILLY JOE SHAVER

(This song originated when I was eight years old. It was one of the first songs I wrote.)

Honey bee, honey bee
You know I love you
Come on darlin' let me hold your little hand
You know I could never put no one above you
Honey bee I want to be your lovin' man

I recall the first day ever I did see her
She was walkin' with her schoolbooks in her arms
When I finally figured out a way to meet her
I was shaking so I could not even talk

Honey bee, honey bee
You know I love you
Come on darlin' let me hold your little hand
You know I could never put no one above you
Honey bee I want to be your lovin' man

She's the sweetest little thing this side of heaven
She's a walking, talking wonder of the world
Someday soon I am gonna reach right out and get her
And honey bee she gonna be my loving girl

Honey bee, honey bee
You know I love you
Come on darlin' let me hold your little hand
You know I could never put no one above you
Honey bee I want to be your lovin' man

RIDE ME DOWN EASY

BY BILLY JOE SHAVER

The highway she's hotter than nine kinds of hell
The rides 'bout as scarce as the rain
When you're down to your last shuck with nothing to sell
And too far away from the trains

Been a good month of Sundays and a guitar ago
Had a tall drink of yesterday's wine
Left a long string of friends, some sheets in the wind
And some satisfied women behind

First Chorus:
Hey ride me down easy Lord ride me on down
Leave word in the dust where I lay
Say I'm easy come, easy go, and
Easy to love when I stay

Put snow on the mountain, raised hell on the hill
Locked horns with the Devil himself
Been a rodeo bum, I'm a son of a gun
And a hobo with stars in my crown

Second Chorus:
Ride me down easy Lord ride me on down
Leave word in the dust where I lay
Say I'm easy come, easy go, and
Easy to love when I stay

I COULDN'T BE ME WITHOUT YOU

BY BILLY JOE SHAVER

I'm putting some new strings on my old guitar
I know just what I'm gonna do
I'm gonna sit down and write me a song
And I'm gonna sing it to you

I realise now after all those hard times
And Lord knows we've had us a few
Together forever wherever we are
I couldn't be me without you

Chorus:
I couldn't be me without you
I couldn't be me without you
Together forever wherever we are
I couldn't be me without you

Repeat Chorus

YESTERDAY TOMORROW IS TODAY

BY BILLY JOE SHAVER

1970, ATV Catalog, administered By EMI-Sony

When the autumn leaves were fallen and the winter winds were callin'
And the southbound geese were chasin' summertime
I was hungry green, and slender as well as I remember
Fighting for a place in life I could call mine

Yesterday tomorrow was today you dreamer
Yesterday tomorrow was today

At the age of five and ten I put a handle on the wind
And learned to travel on the heels of summertime
Like a souped-up '50 Ford down the road of life I roared
Never carin' for a thing I left behind

Yesterday tomorrow was so far away
Yesterday I was runnin' wild and free
Yesterday tomorrow was today young man
Yesterday tomorrow was today

From New York, to L.A., up the San Francisco Bay to the shimmerin'
    Paris lights
And the warm Australian nights
In the honky tonks and bars and the back seats of the cars
I learned my lessons well and I proudly wore my scars

Yesterday tomorrow was a blinding thing
Yesterday tomorrow came so fast
Yesterday tomorrow was today old friend
Yesterday tomorrow came at last

In the solitary gloom of some old lonely hotel room
While struggling for a way to right the wrong
The Savior Jesus Christ came into my life
The old man passed away and the young man lives today

Yesterday tomorrow and today He is the same
Yesterday He washed my sins away
Yesterday tomorrow and today are the same
Yesterday tomorrow is today

WEST TEXAS WALTZ

BY BILLY JOE SHAVER

Published by Suite Two O Five Music / Restless Wind Music (BMI)

He was a honky tonk hero, she was the west Texas rose
He had his hands clinched in hatred and she made the sweet flowers
grow
They met on a Saturday evening at a place called the Last Chance
Saloon
Her hand in his stopped its tremblin' when he laughed as they
danced 'cross the room

The jukebox was playing a beautiful song
A tune called the West Texas Waltz
And it seemed like the whole world was dancing along
With the music controlling it all

Away come away from that window, come lay down beside me a
while
You know I stepped out of the shadows to walk in the warmth of your
smile
Nobody knows me like you do, you changed me and made me your
man
I gave up the life of an outlaw the day that you gave me your hand

He was a honky tonk hero and she was the west Texas rose
They met on a Saturday evening and she made the sweet flowers
grow

HIGHWAY OF LIFE

BY BILLY JOE SHAVER

Published by Suite Two O Five Music / Restless Wind Music (BMI)

On a long winding road just this side of nowhere
A whippoorwill warbles its voice through the night
There's a hungry old hound checkin' sacks in the bar ditch
It's lonesome as hell on the highway of life

Oh the outlaws they ride on their two-wheeled monsters
Like a big giant serpent they glide through the night
Just shakin' their chains like a diamondback rattler
It's dangerous as hell on the highway of life

On the highway of life there will be chances taken
On the highway of life don't you be mistaken
You drive or you ride, you fight or you die
Somehow you survive on the highway of life

There's good and there's bad, a wrong and a right way
A dark and a light day and some in between
So you try to stay straight and you mind your own business
You keep yourself real and you watch what you dream

On the highway of life there will be chances taken
On the highway of life don't you be mistaken
You drive or you ride, you fight or you die
Somehow you survive on the highway of life

Yeah, you keep movin' on on the highway of life

TOMORROW'S GOODBYE

BY BILLY JOE SHAVER

Published by Suite Two O Five Music / Restless Wind Music (BMI)

Tomorrow I'll say goodbye to the woman I thought was mine
As I gracefully leave behind love that come to an end
Tomorrow her memory will become just a part of me
Like a beautiful melody to recall now and then

There's no use pretending I won't miss her at all
With springtime and summer I've accepted the fall
Tomorrow I must forget the warmth of her tender kiss
And the laughter between the tears was like heaven to me

There's no use pretending I won't miss her at all
With springtime and summer I've accepted the fall
Someday I may understand why she wanted another man
But for now I'll stick to my plan and just tell her goodbye

Tomorrow I'll say goodbye to the world that I leave behind
As my journey through life unwinds with tomorrow's goodbye

BLUE BLUE BLUES

BY BILLY JOE SHAVER

Published by Co-Heart Music, Inc. (BMI)

I know you're wonderin' where in the world I been
I look like somethin' the barnyard cats drug in
I got my head hung a-hangin'
And I sure could use a friend

You know I prayed to my God
And my God answered me
I prayed to my God and my God set me free
But I found out too late
Free ain't where I want to be

Blue blue blues, blues all over me
Blue blue blues, blue as I can be
I got the blues for you honey
But you ain't got the blues for me

I'm the one who left you
That's a cold hard natural fact
I throwed my ring in the river
Down yonder by the railroad track
Now I'm back here a beggin' honey please
Won't you take me back

COMIN' ON STRONG

BY BILLY JOE SHAVER

Published by Rage of the Age Music (BMI)

Comin' on strong, comin' on strong
I can feel my love for you comin' on strong
Oh why did I roam, was I gone too long
I can feel my love for you comin' on strong

In my heart I knew I never would forget you
In my mind I know the damage that was done
I've done all I can to try and not upset you
But this feeling in me keeps on comin' on

Comin' on strong, comin' on strong
Oh I pray to God I haven't waited too long
Comin' on strong, comin' on strong
I can feel my love for you comin' on strong

I know you know I've been with other lovers
And I know you've known some too since I've been gone
Maybe miracles are meant to be discovered
Comin' 'round again just like the morning sun

Comin' on strong, comin' on strong
I can feel my love for you comin' on strong
Comin' on strong, comin' back home
I can feel my love for you comin' on strong

YOU'RE AS YOUNG AS THE WOMAN YOU FEEL

BY BILLY JOE SHAVER

Published by Rage of the Age Music (BMI)

You're as young as the woman you feel
If you try you can make time stand still
It's a hell of a heavenly deal
You're as young as the woman you feel

In my heart is an old-fashioned song and it gingerly nudges me on
But it goes spinning head over heels when I'm holding my girlfriend
    Lucille
Now Lucille she just turned twenty-one and she really does turn
    me on
When she hugs me and bounces on my knee she makes a big old
    baby out of me

Willie Nelson likes his women young
Says it helps him write good country songs
When they divorce him he doesn't fight
He just keeps all those great copyrights

You're as young as the woman you feel
If you try you can make time stand still
It's a hell of a heavenly deal
You're as young as the woman you feel

GOODBYE YESTERDAY

BY BILLY JOE SHAVER

1970, ATV (BMI) Sony

Spending time today is the only way to buy a new tomorrow
And I'll agree that you and me have the same price to pay
For nothing sane was ever gained by dwelling in the past
And even fools like me can see forevers seldom last

Goodbye yesterday, goodbye dreams I won't be dreamin'
Goodbye memories of a love I thought was true
Goodbye reasons why I cried all night and wished that I could die
Goodbye yesterday, yesterday goodbye

At the break of day I'll find a way to face the new tomorrow
And with the dawn I'll carry on and I'll have no regrets
Old memories of you and me will fade and pass away
And peace of mind will come in time and save me when I say

Goodbye yesterday, goodbye dreams I won't be dreamin'
Goodbye memories of a love I thought was true
Goodbye reasons why I cried all night and wished that I could die
Goodbye yesterday, yesterday goodbye

MOONSHINE AND INDIAN BLOOD

BY BILLY JOE SHAVER, EDDY SHAVER, TONY COLTON

Published by Warner Chappell Music, Inc. (BMI)
Suite Two O Five Music / Restless Wind Music

She was dang near full-blood Apache
I am a half-breed Cherokee
We did a lot of screaming in the canyon
She was a warrior like me

Some nights when the heat hung heavy
We'd skin down and howl at the moon
But when we started drinkin' fire water
The reason and rhyme left the tune

Stirred up like Texas tornadoes
A wild concoction of love
There ain't no crazier mixture
Than moonshine and Indian blood

We had to spilt the blanket
Or tear each other to shreds
But still every night when I'm sleepin'
I save a place for her in my bed

LOOK FOR ME WHEN YOU SEE ME COMIN'
BY BILLY JOE SHAVER
Published by Rage of the Age Music (BMI)

There's a road outside your window and it's going everywhere
When I packed my bag and hit that road you didn't even care
You thought the one you took up with could take the place of me
Now you're down and out and lookin' out and askin' 'round 'bout me

Look for me when you see me comin'
Your long-lost lover and friend
Look for me when you see me comin'
Look for me if you see me again

When that cold north wind starts howlin' and your fair-weather
    friends are gone
When the only one you counted on has left you all alone
Just remember the way you done me and the trail of tears I cried
And remember I'll always love you and I'll see you by and by

Look for me when you see me comin'
Your long-lost lover and friend
Look for me when you see me comin'
Look for me if you see me again

THE FIRST AND LAST TIME

BY BILLY JOE SHAVER

Co-Published by Restless Wind Music (BMI) and Justice Artists Music Corp. (BMI)

The very first time I fell in love was the first and last time for me
Her and the moon and the stars up above, how could I be so naive
Of all the hard lessons I've learned in my life, the one that stays
    closest to me
Is I was in love but she didn't love me, I was too blind to see

She was a wonderful dancer
She'd glide in and out of my door
I was just one of her partners
The one who kept beggin' for more

Love doesn't come with a handle you turn
Love can't be turned off or on
So you roll with the punches and laugh while it's there
And cry in your beer when it's gone

The very first time she said goodbye
Was the last time she cared for me
She still comes around to rattle my chains
And make sure that I'm never free

She's still a wonderful dancer
Sometimes she glides through my door
I used to be one of her partners
The one who's still beggin' for more

The very first time I fell in love
Was the first and last time for me

SON OF CALVARY
BY BILLY JOE SHAVER

The crayon-colored oceans
Wash into the fading sky
There to tremble into darkness
Like a bird about to die

O so gentle in all oneness
Is creation blessed to be
O so fathomless in beauty
O so physical in need

From the splitting of an atom
To the driving of a nail
From the grandness of the Tetons
To a prison's mental hell

No word can describe
Free feeling full eternity
From the dawning of creation
Born in all humanity

When my day on earth has ended
And the race is overrun
I will melt into the likeness
Of my own beloved ones

Lord I fear for gentle shelter
O so tender am I now
Silent sacred solitude how it knits
Upon my brow

Blessed be the Son of Calvary
Blessed be this gift to you and me

COWBOY WHO STARTED THE FIGHT
BY BILLY JOE SHAVER

The legs on the lady a-walkin'
Was tanned to a dark berry brown
Her body was made like a song to be played
To the tune of a million a pound

She was a wonder of a woman I reckon
And she's who screwed her head on right
The toast of the world was the long-legged girl
And the cowboy who started the fight

Well he had just pulled into town in a beat up old green
    1953 Chevrolet pickup truck
With whisky bumps all over it and the right front fender fallin' off
He coasted into a no parking zone
Got out and took his keys and chunked 'em down a gutter
Then turned around and just walked off

He allowed how his time had been wasted
On drinking and running around
He spent half his life searching barrooms at night
For the sweetheart that he never found

It was plain from the moment their eyes met
They'd wind up in each others arms
The lady's young life was laid open that night
And the cowboy drank deep of her charms

Singing hey hidy hee, from the depths of the sea
To the mountains so hollering high
He'd found the best one under God's given sun
Yeah, the cowboy got lucky that night

While the angel beside him lay sleepin'
He silently thanked God above
For being a kind-hearted father
And blessing his life with her love

For one night of love with that woman
Was more than he knew he deserved
So he found all he had left worth givin'
And he gave all he had left to her

He slid back inside his old Wranglers
And filled up his boots with his feet
While the subways beneath New York City
Screamed through the veins of the street

Yeah, the lady gave up without question
The trophy she'd saved all her life
Then she curled up beside his old weatherworn hide
When the cowboy just laid down and died

Hey, hidy hee, went a whoop through the street
As his soul slowly winged out of sight
The lady lived on for the child to be born
And the cowboy found heaven that night

I'M IN LOVE

BY BILLY JOE SHAVER

From the deepness of night
I have awakened to my vanity, Oh why
Have I all these years
Suffered this insanity, thank God
I can see you really live inside me
I'm in love

For the first and the last
And the only time I'll ever
I have been born again
And the cord is finally severed, I am free
To begin the beginning of forever
I'm in love

I'm in love
I'm in love
And I know I know I know I know it
You're the angel of light
You have sewn the seed and grown it, for the rest
Of my life I can never keep from glowin'
I'm in love
I'm in love

CHRISTIAN SOLDIER

BY BILLY JOE SHAVER

Not so long ago in Oklahoma
The son of an Okie preacher knelt to pray
He said "Lord I wanna be a Christian soldier just for you
And fight to build a new and better day"

Now many years and miles from Oklahoma
That same young Okie boy still kneels to pray
But he don't pray to be no Christian soldier anymore
He just prays to make it through another day

'Cause Lord it's hard to be a Christian soldier when you tote a gun
And it hurts to have to watch a grown man cry
But we're playin' cards and writin' home and havin' lots of fun
Tellin' jokes and learnin' how to die

The things I've come to know seem so confusin'
It's gettin' hard anymore to tell what's wrong from right
I can't separate the winnin' from the losin' anymore
So I'm thinkin' bout just givin' up the fight

'Cause Lord it's hard to be a Christian soldier when you tote a gun
And it hurts to have to watch a grown man cry
But we're playin' cards and lightin' up and ain't we havin' fun
Turnin' on and learnin' how to die

MY MOTHER'S NAME IS VICTORY

BY BILLY JOE SHAVER

My pappy was a roughhouse rounder
My mother's name is Victory
I'm bound to win this whole world over
For Jesus Christ who lives in me

Full well I know I am a sinner
Full well I know my Savior's name
From where I stand he lives within us
'Til one in all, we are the same

When Jesus comes in all His glory
We will meet Him in the sky
Through modern times old gospel stories
Explain the way and reasons why

Oh yes there is a higher highway
Yes there is peace beyond the shore
When we have grown into His likeness
We'll rise and walk through Heaven's door

My pappy was a roughhouse rounder
My mother's name is Victory

PRESENTS FROM THE PAST

BY BILLY JOE SHAVER

Presents from the past
Go floating in and out in time
Till they come resting like a snowflake
Falling on this heart of mine

Oh what a peaceful kind of payment
For all the joy we feel inside
Yes there is no doubt about it
It's here it's really Christmas time

Then you're looking at a stranger
For just a moment 'til you find
He is the reason for your happiness
He is the brightest star you'll find

Presents from the past
You are a child again at last
Christ is born again in every heart He's born again
Presents from the past

THE BOW AND THE ARROW
BY BILLY JOE SHAVER

My only son, my precious one
Come listen here to me
I am the bow and you are the arrow
And now you must fly free

The bow is bent so the arrow is sent
On its long and graceful flight
And the path you make will become your fate
God is on your side

I know someday the human race
Will find a better world
In a galaxy where the sky and trees
Are the same as those on earth

The fate of man will be in the hands
Of the strong and chosen few
When you reach this place through time and space
We all depend on you

My only son, my precious one
Come listen here to me
I am the bow and you are the arrow
And now you must fly free

TRY AND TRY AGAIN

BY BILLY JOE SHAVER

Well I went up on the mountain
And I looked down on my life
I had squandered all my money
Lost my son and wife
My heart was filled with sorrow
And I almost took my life
But I found the strength inside me
To give life one more try.

If at first you don't succeed, try and try again
If at first you don't succeed, just try and try again
If all you do is lose you better find a way to win
If at first you don't succeed try and try again.

I know someday the world will learn
To sing a better song
The lame will walk, the mute will talk
We all will sing along
The fighting will be ended
And all hunger will be gone
It's everybody's business
'Til we get the good work done.

If at first you don't succeed, try and try again
If at first you don't succeed, just try and try again
If all you do is lose you better find a way to win
If at first you don't succeed try and try again.

I know someday, I say I know someday
The deaf man's gonna hear the blind man's song
And someday the whole world's gonna grow new ears
To hear and new eyes to see and we're all gonna sing along
Yes we will and our point of view is gonna
grow into a pure and perfect one
And the voice of truth inside us all is gonna
help us sing that song
If at first you don't succeed brother, sister
Just try and try and try again
Amen and amen

LEANIN' T'WARD THE BLUES

BY BILLY JOE SHAVER

Lazy loafin' good for nothing no count knock around
Ain't been worth a honky damn since country came to town
I'll tell you boys this working up to somethin'
Got me down to nothin' left to lose
Lately I been leanin' t'ward the blues

Lately I been leanin' t'ward the blues
I been leanin' lately t'ward the blues
Done held on to it 'til I can't turn loose

Everything is everything everybody knows
We can't get nowhere by steppin' on each other's toes
And when it comes to cuttin' corners honey
Anyway you get here is just fine
Lately we been pickin' double time

Lately I been leanin' t'ward the blues
I been leanin' lately t'ward the blues
Done wore a sole in my old holy shoes
You got it all now.

NEW YORK CITY

BY BILLY JOE SHAVER

New York City, oh what a town
I can't wait to get my feet on your ground
I been around a time or two and I've found
Ain't nothing like the likes of you
You got your big tall buildings
They scrape the sky
Way up yonder where the eagles fly
Boy you really made me open up my eyes
And all I want to see is you

If you walk down on Broadway and 42nd Avenue
Ain't no telling who you'll see
And ain't no tellin' what they'll do
You've got the prettiest women I've ever seen
Checkered cabs and long limousines
The hustle and bustle is music to me
Buddy won't you play me some more
Play some more now

Oh those moonlight nights in Manhattan
With my New York City girl
That nail I hang my hat on
Is the best there is all over this world

Oh New York City, oh what a town
I can't wait to get my feet on your ground
I been around a time or two and I've found
Ain't nothing like the likes of you
You got your big tall buildings
They scrape the sky
Way up yonder where the eagles fly
Boy you really made me open up my eyes
And all I want to see is you.

YOU WOULDN'T KNOW LOVE (IF YOU FELL IN IT)
BY BILLY JOE SHAVER AND JOHN YOUNG

I fell in love with you in a New York minute
Down in San Antonio, baby at our second beginning
I was so happy-go-lucky in love with you
Now your mood has changed
Back to the same old thing
You're poutin' and doubtin' and runnin' around on me again
I don't know too much baby
But this much I know about you

You wouldn't know love if you fell in it
You didn't break my heart this time
But you dang sure bent it
You wouldn't know love
Oh you wouldn't know love if you fell it

Before the second time I fell for you
You swore you'd stop lying and being untrue
I should've known by then that some people never change
Now the truth has come to set me free
And the truth is baby, you never loved me
I've been deaf, dumb and blind girl
But now I finally see

You wouldn't know love
You didn't break my heart this time
But you put a big old dent in it
You wouldn't know love
Oh you wouldn't know love if you fell it

SLAVE AT THE FEET OF THE QUEEN

BY BILLY JOE SHAVER

Oh you know I will always love you
Even though you have proven untrue
In your own way I know that you still love me too
You're the reason I'm singing the blues

With these holes in my soul and my shoes
I am known as the King of the Blues
For a lifetime of sorrow and suffering I've seen
I'm just a slave at the feet of the queen

I'm just a slave at the feet of the queen
And I know I will never be free
I am shackled to your love and you hold the key
I'm just a slave at the feet of the queen

When my life on this old world is through
I will go to my grave loving you
A scarred-up old warrior who paid all his dues
Just a loser with nothing to lose

I'm just a slave at the feet of the queen
And I know I will never be free
I am shackled to your love and you hold the key
I'm just a slave at the feet of the queen.

PEOPLE AND THEIR PROBLEMS
BY BILLY JOE SHAVER

My sister's kid is tattooed from his head down to his toes
He claims trouble follows him everywhere he goes
He's such a lazy loafin' good for nothin' drunken slob
But still he thinks I ought to give his sorry ass a job

People and their problems are giving me a pain
People and their problems are messing with my brain
I try to help 'em solve 'em
But they always stay the same
People and their problems are driving me insane

The President stays pissed off with the Congress and the House
It takes 'em half a year to try and figure something out
Republicans and Democrats have parties on TV
Then raise the taxes high as Hell on folks like you and me

Yeah people and their problems are giving me a pain
People and their problems are messing with my brain
I try to help 'em solve 'em
But they always stay the same
People and their problems are driving me insane

Ol' Willie he stays higher than a hundred-dollar kite
He huffs and puffs and smokes that stuff every day and night
His friends all try to change him, begging please quit Willie, please
But still they hang around and breathe the same air that he breathes

Yeah people and their problems are giving me a pain
People and their problems are messing with my brain
I try to help 'em solve 'em
But they always stay the same
People and their problems are driving me insane.

I'LL BE HERE
BY BILLY JOE SHAVER

Come on honey, take my hand
Let me help you understand
I will always be in love with you
I'll stand by you, wrong or right
Every day and every night
I'm just hoping you feel the same way too

I'll be here, I'll be here
I ain't going anywhere
I'll be here as long as you want me to be
You're my woman, I'm your man
I'm your lover and your friend
I'll be here, I ain't goin' anywhere

From the moment we first met, until I draw my final breath
You will always be the only one for me
You're my first love and my last
You're my future and my past
I'll be here, I ain't goin' anywhere

I'll be here, I'll be here
I ain't going anywhere
I'll be here as long as you want me to be
You're my woman, I'm your man
I'm your lover and your friend
I'll be here, I ain't goin' anywhere.
I'll be here, I ain't goin' anywhere.

WAY DOWN TEXAS WAY

BY BILLY JOE SHAVER

Adios goodbye amigos, I am leaving you today
Ain't nobody 'round this town that's gonna miss me anyway
This ol' money makin's takin' all my time I have to play
Momma hush your mouth, I'm headin' south
Way down Texas way

Way down Texas way they play good music every night
And the dance halls ring with laughter 'til the early mornin' light
And when them cowboys get through pickin', they ain't much that's
    left to say
You can really have a good time, honey
Way down Texas way

The road of life is paved with good intentions I am told
So I best be on my way now or I may not ever go
Ain't no need to be beggin' me to stay just one more day
This old wild goose is cuttin' loose
Way down Texas way

Way down Texas way they play good music every night
And the dance halls ring with laughter 'til the early mornin' light
When them cowboys get through pickin', they ain't much that's left
    to say
You can really have a good time, sugar
Way down Texas way

SHE CAN DANCE

BY BILLY JOE SHAVER

The day she was born, down on the farm
She could bend like a young willow tree
And she started singing and dancing around
At the ripe old age of three

She'd sing and she'd dance
Every time she got the chance
She just could not be controlled
And she started stepping out late at night
When she was just thirteen years old

She could dance, Lord God she could dance
She just danced her young life away
From dusk 'til dawn, 'til the cows come home
As long as the music would play
Yeah she could dance, Lord God she could dance
She just danced her young life away

She was sweet sixteen when she run into me
It was down at the Panther Hall
She kicked off her shoes and was dancing the blues
It was the dangdest thing you ever saw
She could dance, Lord God she could dance
She just danced my heart away

I made her my wife, and she danced through my life
Like a whirlwind in a storm
We sashayed around from town to town
'Cause she didn't give a hoot about the farm

She can dance, Lord God she can dance
She's still dancin' my heart away
From dusk 'til dawn, 'til the cows come home
As long as the music will play
She can dance, Lord God she can dance
She's still dancin' 'til this very day
She can dance, Lord God she can dance
She's still dancin' my heart away.

Yeah she could dance, Lord God she could dance
She just danced her young life away

LOVE IS SO SWEET
BY BILLY JOE SHAVER

I've been around this world a long time mister
I got a thing or two to say
Don't wanna bore you with no tough tongue twister
You wouldn't buy that anyway

Love is so sweet
It makes you bounce when you walk down the street

You've been to school
You say you are a lawyer
You walked out of a magazine
I've been a drifter and a low-life loser
You could learn a lot from me

I've got to say I have looked
At life a whole 'nother way
Yes, and love is so sweet
It makes you bounce when you walk down the street

One thing in common is we all are different
We're supposed to be that way
Live and let live is such a good reminder
You'd do well to be that way

I've got to say
I have looked at life a whole 'nother way
Yes, and love is so sweet
It makes you bounce when you walk down the street

Love is so sweet
It makes you bounce when you walk down the street
Love is so sweet
It makes you bounce when you walk down the street
Love is so sweet
It makes you bounce when you walk down the street

HARD HEADED HEART

BY BILLY JOE SHAVER

You sure have got a hard headed heart
You good for nothing, son of a gun
You're always out there running through them honky tonks and bars
And never winding up with anyone
You're almost down to nothing left to lose
Your way of life has told a tell on you
There's a little girl in Texas wondering where you are
You sure have got a hard headed heart

A Hard Headed heart ain't hard to come by
Just like a frog slides off a log
You drop down to your knees easy as you please
'Til you can't remember what you're falling for
Then you take another drink to keep from trying
Like the foolish fool that you are
You low-down rascal you, you were born to live the blues
You sure have got a hard headed heart

You sure have got a hard headed heart
You good for nothing, son of a gun
You're always out there running through them honky tonks and bars
And never winding up with anyone
You're almost down to nothing left to lose
Your way of life has told a tell on you
There's a little girl in Texas wondering where you are
You sure have got a hard headed heart

NEW YORK CITY GIRL
BY BILLY JOE SHAVER

I've traveled these United States from shore to shore for sure
And every girl I've left just left me reaching out for more
And then I met this New York gal down at O'Looney's Bar
No matter where I've been since then, my heart stayed with her there

My New York City girl, my New York City girl
She sparkles like a diamond and her heart is pure as pearl
Beats everything I've ever seen around this whole wide world
There ain't no 'nother other like my New York City girl

She looked and sounded like an Irish angel sitting there
A flaming halo glowing all around her auburn hair
She played the guitar like it was a man between her knees
And every other song she sang she'd dedicate to me

My New York City girl, my New York City girl
She sparkles like a diamond and her heart is pure as pearl
Beats everything I've ever seen around this whole wide world
There ain't no 'nother other like my New York City girl.

There ain't no 'nother other like my New York City girl.

SAIL OF MY SOUL
BY BILLY JOE SHAVER

I know you're there, but I don't care
Which a way you're comin' from
Or how you're gettin' where
They chunked me out of the place
And I can't buy me no booze
You know it hurts me from my head
Plumb down to the sole of my boots

Sail of my soul, sail of my soul
Catch me some wind yeah
And save me some row
I said sail of my soul
Ever-loving sail of my soul
Won't you catch me some wind yeah
And save me from this doggone row

Sweet Joycey mine, you know you're fine honey
Taste a whole bunch better than that homemade cherry pie
Ain't a woman no, can love me all over like you do girl
You changed the locks on your place babe
And I can't face up to them blues

Sail of my soul, sail of my soul
Catch me some wind now
And save me this row
I said sail of my soul
Ever-loving sail of my soul
Won't you catch me some wind yeah
And save me some of this doggone row

YOU'RE TOO MUCH FOR ME
BY BILLY JOE SHAVER

I can't take any more
You're too much for me
Go find someone new
Just let me be
You got places to go
And people to see
Leave while you can
Don't worry about me

I got a few precious friends
And a measure of pride
I can live without you
Yes, I will survive
Have fun with yourself
Be wild and free
I can't take any more
You're too much for me

In my life and time
I've been such a fool
I gave all that I had
To people like you
I got work I must do
And debts I must pay
I got a reason to live
I can't throw life away

I got a few precious friends
And a measure of pride
I can live without you
Yes, I will survive
Have fun with yourself
Be wild and free
I can't take any more
You're too much for me

I can't take any more
You're too much for me

BLOOD IS THICKER THAN WATER
BY BILLY JOE SHAVER AND EDDY SHAVER

You come dancing in here with the devil's daughter
Spilling beer and doing things you hadn't oughta
You found her walkin' the streets carryin' a sack of quarters
Now she's stealing rings off the hands of your dying mother
If that witch don't leave I believe I'm gonna have to help her
Don't you know that blood, blood is thicker than water
Blood is thicker than water

In the mother's heart are so many sons and daughters
When the water breaks, they wash out into the world
They're the tie that binds between the mothers and the fathers
I know that blood, blood is thicker than water
Blood is thicker than water

Can't you see I'm down to the ground, I can't get no lower
I've seen you puking out your guts and running with sluts
When you was married to my mother
Now the powers that be are leading you and me like two lambs to the
    slaughter
I need a friend, I'm your son, and you're always gonna be my father
Don't you know that blood, blood is thicker than water
Blood is thicker than water

When the thief arrives we won't even know what hit us
And the blood of Christ will be spilled throughout the world
And the born again, all the children of the Father
Will be drawn as one to the living well of life
And the hand of God will bring creation back to order
I tell you blood, blood is thicker than water
Blood is thicker than water

STAR IN MY HEART
BY BILLY JOE SHAVER

You'll have to do the best you can good friend of mine
Someday our paths may cross again in a better time
I know, you know, you know, you know that
I pulled the thorn out of your side when I walked away
I took the rock out of your shoe on that very day
I pray, you'll forgive me for not leaving sooner

You are the star in my heart
Guess you've always known
Though we are many worlds apart
I'm still your friend
And friends will always be friends forever

Don't waste your precious thoughts on me and my tired old dreams
Your soul is bursting at the seams, you are finally free, to be
Even more than you could ever dream of
You'll learn to hold your head up high and you'll make your stand
You'll look the world straight in the eye, you will never blink
To think I almost held on too long to help you

You are the star in my heart
Guess you've always known
Though we are many worlds apart
I'm still your friend
And friends will always be friends forever

You are the star in my heart
Guess you've always known
Though we are many worlds apart
I'm still your friend
And friends will always be friends forever

You are the star in my heart

IT'S NOT OVER 'TIL IT'S OVER

BY BILLY JOE SHAVER

It's not over 'til it's over and it's not over yet

I've seen you in the mirror everyday since you've left home
And I've watched you slowly losin' what it takes to carry on
I've heard your hollow laughter, heard you say what's done is done
While the one you left behind you is sadly waiting all alone

It's not over 'til it's over and it's not over yet
Did you think someone who loves you would be that easy to forget
Everyday since you left her you've known nothing but regret
It's not over 'til it's over and it's not over yet

You go out to the nightclubs and you try and have some fun
You tip your glass of laughter and you drink 'em one by one
But you wind-up thinking about her when you wake up all alone
And you feel so sick and sorry for the damage you have done

It's not over 'til it's over and it's not over yet
Did you think someone who loves you would be that easy to forget
Everyday since you left her you've known nothing but regret
It's not over 'til it's over and it's not over yet

It's not over 'til it's over and it's not over yet

Give her a call dumbass

HEARTS A-BUSTIN'

BY BILLY JOE SHAVER

Hearts a-bustin' grew down by the river
That flows by the old paper mill
In the springtime we stood there together
At the top of the old stone fort hill

Many's a-time I've been lonesome
Since you left I don't know what to do
Like the flower that grows on the hillside
My hearts a-bustin' for you

Hearts a-bustin' is a beautiful flower
That looks like its heart burst inside
I miss you so much, your sweet gentle touch
I'll love you 'til the day that I die

One day in the year when the time's right
The Indians float 'round the bend
I don't know when I'll go but somehow I know
Someday I'll be with you again

Hearts a-bustin' grew down by the river
That flows by the old paper mill
In the springtime we stood there together
At the top of the old stone fort hill.

LEAVIN' AMARILLO

BY BILLY JOE SHAVER

Sometimes I want to hug her
Sometimes I want to wring her neck
She wants to be a big star
But she can't even sing a lick
She's got an ass about thirteen axe-handles wide
And to stay here with her would be suicide
So I'm leavin' Amarillo and I ain't coming back again.

Screw you, you ain't worth passing through
Hey hey, you don't route anyway
What more can I say

I'm down at the station, just tryin' to buy some gasoline
I'm leavin' Amarillo and I ain't coming back again
You can't buy beer here at the grocery store
But I won't have to worry about that no more
'Cause I'm leavin' Amarillo and I ain't a-coming' back again.

Screw you, you ain't worth passing through
Hey hey, you don't route anyway
What more can I say

There's a whole bunch of cookie cutters waitin' up in Tennessee
They're makin' stars everyday and one of 'em could be me
I may keep my old hat and learn to sing through my nose
And I may even buy me some sequined clothes
But I'm leavin' Amarillo and I ain't a-coming back again.

Screw you, you ain't worth passing through
Hey hey, you don't route anyway
What more can I say.

Recitation:
I tell you what, every time we ever played Amarillo they paid us with
a check that bounced like a basketball. So we ain't playin' there no
more. They ain't nothin' between Amarillo and the north pole but a
barbed wire fence, and it's down. I'm telling you it's just a big insane
asylum and nobody knows how to leave. To your left there is Lubbock. There's some good folks in Lubbock but they're all dead. If we
went back to Amarillo, they'd probably lynch us, but they ain't got no
trees. So screw you Amarillo very much.

I DON'T SEEM TO FIT ANYWHERE
BY BILLY JOE SHAVER

Just like this old rocking chair
I move but I'm gettin' nowhere
A junked out old caisson too worn from the wear
Too thin to be used as a spare

My dreams of a lifetime are gone
Old friends that I once counted on
Nobody quite got the drift of my songs
Like me they're a bit overdone

And I don't seem to fit anywhere
Just like these old clothes that I wear
I feel 'bout as short as the length of my hair
And I don't seem to fit anywhere

These new-fangled folks now-a-days
They laugh at my old-fashioned ways
I may have done better if I learned not to care
'Cause I don't seem to fit anywhere

I don't seem to fit anywhere
Just like these old clothes that I wear
I feel 'bout as short as the length of my hair
And I don't seem to fit anywhere

THE EARTH ROLLS ON
BY BILLY JOE SHAVER

The earth rolls on, the earth rolls on
The earth rolls on and on and on
The pale moonlight shines through the night
And slowly fades into the dawn
It was you, who swore that you loved me
And it was you, who stole my heart away
Yes it's true, it's true I will love you
'Til tomorrow rolls away

The earth rolls on, the earth rolls on
Through the sunshine and the rain
The seasons come and the seasons go
The seasons come and go again
Just a falling star from the heaven
With its silent disappearing light
Yes it's true, it's true I will love you
'Til the earth rolls out of sight

The earth rolls on, even though you're gone
The earth rolls on and on and on

HOLD ON TO YOURS AND I'LL HOLD ON TO MINE

BY BILLY JOE SHAVER

(BMI)

Sometimes lovers get too close to understand
It takes space to be a woman or a man
So they both bend until they nearly break
And they think that love is just a big mistake

Chorus:
Hold on to yours and I'll hold on to mine
We don't have to give up either cup of wine
The bottle here is full enough for two
It will last as long as there's a me and you

I'm an old-fashioned person don't you know
I am sure that love is pure as driven snow
So just be yourself and I'll keep being me
If we're lucky we'll be blind enough to see

Repeat Chorus:
Put your hands anywhere they want to be
You can let you fingers walk all over me
If we must to trust we'll drop our guards tonight
If we're wrong we've still got time to make it right

Repeat Chorus

FREEDOM'S CHILD

BY BILLY JOE SHAVER
Sony / ATV Music (BMI)

At the breaking of the dawn, day is born again
Just another missing link in an endless chain
Filling up the empty space left by one who's gone
Freedom's child was born today singing freedom's song

With his colors flying high and his gun in hand
Volunteered to fight and die in a foreign land
Just another minor chord in a worn-out song
Freedom's child is marching there singing freedom's song

Drifting through a crowded park past an empty swing
Hidden in a sparrow's eye when it's on the wing
Planted on a lonely hill with his name unknown
Freedom's child was laid to rest singing freedom's song

At the breaking of the dawn, day is born again
Just another missing link in an endless chain
Filling up the empty space left by one who's gone
Freedom's child was born today singing freedom's song

Tag:
Freedom's child was laid to rest singing freedom's song

THAT'S WHY THE MAN IN BLACK SINGS THE BLUES
BY BILLY JOE SHAVER
(BMI)

There's a drug dealer selling to your children every day
He's rotten evil but he ain't nobody's fool
He's dealing death and living high off your hard-earned pay
That's why the man in black sings the blues

First Chorus:
That's why the man in black sings the blues
Why should children, why should women be abused
There's so precious few among us
Walking in the Savior's shoes
That's why the man in black sings the blues

We've got to stamp out hunger all around the planet earth
We've got to beat our weapons into plows
We've got to ban these bombs I say
We've got to save our lives
We've got to do it all starting now

Second Chorus:
That's why the man in black sings the blues
Why the farmer and his crops worth saving too
So every working stiff across this land won't have to lose
That's why the man in black sings the blues

The first Americans were the red-skinned human beings
They saved us all that first Thanksgiving day
Like the older folks behind walkin' in the welfare line
Their trail of tears grows longer by the way

That's why the man in black sings the blues
Why should children, why should women be abused
There's so precious few among us
Walking in the Savior's shoes
That's why the man in black sings the blues

Tag:
That's why the man in black sang the blues

HONEY CHILE

BY BILLY JOE SHAVER

(BMI)

Honey Chile was a Cajun gal what lived in Vacherie
She stole away my heart there,
But loving don't come free like Honey Chile's

Honey Chile all my friends told me three times or two
I can't make you love me, I can't make you be true, Honey Chile

I didn't know as I paddled up this river yesterday
That a fast-talking gambler would come
And steal away my Honey Chile

Honey Chile, why'd you go and done me that way
Why'd you leave me cryin' on the levee that day Honey Chile

Honey Chile, I done told you if you leave me, don't look back
I'll done you like them crawfish,
Put you in a burlap sack, Honey Chile

I searched 'til I found you in that house in New Orleans
You was trompin' on my heart there,
Being anybody's queen, Honey Chile

You didn't know when we left there headed back to Vacherie
That the ones we left behind us
Had seen all there was to see of Honey Chile

Honey Chile, as I paddle up this river looking back
I see a bump on the levee,
I'm missing one burlap sack and Honey Chile

THE GOOD OL' USA

BY BILLY JOE SHAVER

(BMI)

In the good ol' USA I'm proud to say
We got brand new action, good old fashioned too
And the future so bright like stars in the night
Just smiling down on everything we do

The great big harvest moon beams a happy lover's tune
While sweethearts promenade two by two
Look at you, look at me, we're as lucky as can be
We got a hold of something here worth holding to
Yeah, the USA is made for me and you

In the good ol' USA I'd just like to say
Tomorrow's dreams are always comin' true
And the whole blessed world all the little boys and girls
Are countin' on the old red, white, and blue

We've got faith in the Lord, we got Chevrolets and Fords
We got folks workin' hard to see us through
All the people of the earth
Are gonna get their money's worth
By bettin' on the land of the free
Yeah, the USA is here for you and me

Repeat fourth verse

Tag:
Yeah, the USA is made for you and me

DAY BY DAY

BY BILLY JOE SHAVER

He was twenty and one years the day they were married
She was a young girl just turned seventeen
Her belly was swelled with the child that she carried
The unwelcome start of a God-given dream

Day by day their love kept on growing
Their light kept on glowing and shining so bright
There's hope for the lovers that God draws together
If they hang on 'til everything turns out all right

While the young man broke horse and worked at the sawmill
The young girl would sing to the baby inside
She'd sing him the blues and some rock-n-roll music
Then drift off to sleep with a sweet lullaby

Day by day their love kept on growing
Their light kept on glowing as the years flew on by
There's hope for the family that God holds together
If they hang on 'til everything turns out all right

His fingers would glide 'cross the frets of the guitar
Like slivers of light cross an azure blue sky
The father and son with the prayers of the mother
Still grew in the glow of the heavenly light

Day by day their love kept on growing
Burning and churning through echoes of light
The young girl went home to her heavenly Father
While the husband and son sang the mother good-by

There's many a moonbeam got lost in the forest
And many a forest got burnt to the ground
The son went with Jesus to be with his mother
The father just fell to his knees on the ground

Day by day his heart kept on breaking
And aching to fly to his home in the sky
But now he's arisen from the flames of the forest
With songs from the family that never will die

Day by day their love keeps on growing
Their light keeps on growing and glowing so bright
There's hope for the family that God holds together
'Til they all meet again in the sweet by and by

WE

BY BILLY JOE SHAVER

Me, I could have been the king
I could have had the golden ring
I could have given it to you

You, you could have been the queen
And had the world laid at your feet
You could have saved the world for me

Chorus:
We were so innocent and free
You know we tried our best to be
We had all of everything
Until I gave my love to you
Until you gave your love to me

Life is such a hard old thing to face
When foolishly we break every vow we ever made
Dreams that yesterday were so great
Oh so quickly start to fade
Into a shade of bitter blue

We were so innocent and free
You know we tried our best to be
We had all of everything
Until I gave my love to you
Until you gave your love to me

Tag:
Life is such a hard old thing to face
When foolishly we break every vow we ever made

WILD COW GRAVY

BY BILLY JOE SHAVER
(BMI)

Purt' near all my kinfolk come from up in Arkansas
They's so doggone many of 'em I can't start to count 'em all
When us kids would all get hungry
We'd hunt down a momma cow
We'd head and heel and milk her
I'm gonna tell you how

Aunt Claudie she would duck walk
Right up to that wild milk cow
A fruit jar in her hand, I can almost see her now
It was udderly divine the way she filled that fruit jar up
It didn't look like much, but it was always just enough

Eatin' wild cow gravy and drinkin' mountain dew
It's good enough for me by goll' it's good enough for you
It'll make you live forever even if you don't want to
Eatin' wild cow gravy and drinkin' mountain dew

Black strap molasses and some good Norwegian bread
Will swell your belly up and fill your pencil full of lead
But eatin' wild cow gravy and drinkin' mountain dew
Will make you live forever even if you don't want to

I scratch my head and wonder how'd I come to live this long
After all the reckless ramblin' and the crazy stuff I've done
But eatin' wild cow gravy and drinkin' mountain dew
Will make you live forever even if you don't want to

DRINKIN' BACK

BY BILLY JOE SHAVER

(BMI)

Hello barroom, my old friend
Yeah, it's me, I'm drunk again
Like I've been ever since she went away
I'm just drinkin' back the part
That used to be my heart, 'cause after all
I just drank it away

Yeah. I'm drinkin' back the memory
Of a sweet little woman
So, Mr. Bartender, please let me stay
I've already drank back about a year ago this Monday
She'll be mine Tuesday
If I can drink back yesterday

A little girl I drank away got hung up in yesterday
I didn't know time could move by this fast
Now, yesterday seems far away
Life just moved up another day
So, I'm just thinking Lord and drinkin' back the past

Yeah. I'm drinkin' back the memory
Of a sweet little woman
So, Mr. Bartender, please let me stay
I've already drank back about a year ago this Monday
She'll be mine Tuesday
If I can drink back yesterday

Tag:
She'll be mine Tuesday if I can drink back yesterday

CORSICANA DAILY SUN

BY BILLY JOE SHAVER

(BMI)

It seems like a hundred years
Since I reached out to dry those tears
Streaming down my Grandma's face
When I told her good-bye
She helped me pack her old suitcase
Then pushed my new straw hat in place
When that Corsicana daily sun was shining bright for me

When that sweet smell of youth was mixed
With Grandma's apple pie
What I'd give for a slice of yesterday
When that warm light came splashing 'cross
Those clovered fields of time
And that Corsicana daily sun was shining bright for me

There ain't much that's left to tell
'Cause boy, I really went to hell
It seems like everything went wrong
Since I left my hometown
I wish that I was back there now
Mending fence and milking cows
When Corsicana daily sun was shining bright for me

Recitation:
Someday I'll find that clover bed and I'll lay down
My weary head and watch them soft clouds
Drifting as they tease that country sun
I'll eat a chunk of Grandma's pie
And take a walk back to the time
When Corsicana daily sun was shining bright for me

When that sweet smell of youth was mixed
With Grandma's apple pie
What I'd give for a slice of yesterday
When that warm light came splashing 'cross
Those clovered fields of time
And that Corsicana daily sun was shining bright for me
And that Corsicana daily sun was shining bright for me

THAT'S WHAT SHE SAID LAST NIGHT

BY BILLY JOE SHAVER AND EDDY SHAVER
(BMI)

That's what she said last night
That's what she said last night
You're gonna get it all night all right
That's what she said last night

I went down to Kinko's to get some faxin' done
My ex-girlfriend works down there, she was my number one
She said Billy I'm busy why don't you come around back
I'll clear the store and lock the doors and we can fax all night

That's what she said last night
That's what she said last night
We can fax all night all right
That's what she said last night

I had my other girlfriend staying at my house
When I got home two days late she up and chunked me out
I went and bought her this Gruen watch
To make things up with her
She said Billy I love a good Gruen then she began to purr

That's what she said last night
That's what she said last night
I love a real good Gruen all right all night
That's what she said last night

I got a brand new cell phone, AT&T
It was a little bitty thing just right for a country boy like me
My girlfriend took a poke at the thing and then she threw it away
She said Billy I know you're attached to that thing
But it's too small for me

That's what she said last night
That's what she said last night
That little things too small for me
That's what she said last night

Recitation:
I tell you what, next time I get one of them cell phones, it's gonna be
a big old good un that vibrates and glows in the dark. You just can't
seem to please these women nowadays. They want it bigger and better. Some of 'em like the black model, bigger and better, bigger and
better, yellow models, red models . . .

DEJA BLUES

BY BILLY JOE SHAVER AND TODD SNIDER
(BMI)

I got the deja blues
She said to take your money and stick it
Where the sun don't shine
Pack up your stuff and stay away from mine
Get your hands off of me and move on down the line

I got the deja blues all over again
I got the deja blues y'all, all over again
I just lose and lose
Lord, I just can't seem to win

Well, the bossman said he had to let me go last night
So I went out drinkin' and I got into a fight
I saw the left one comin'
But he caught me with the right

I got the deja blues all over again
I got the deja blues y'all, all over again
I just lose and lose
Lord, I just can't seem to win

Well the police come and they hauled me off to jail
I called up my woman and she wouldn't even go my bail
When it comes to losin' I just can't seem to fail
Aw Hell

I got the deja blues all over again
I got the deja blues y'all, all over again
I just lose and lose
Lord, I just can't seem to win

MAGNOLIA MOTHER'S LOVE
BY BILLY JOE SHAVER
(BMI)

I recall the day she found it
Came home with her coat wrapped around it
Back when I was just a little boy

I'd have sworn that it was dead
But it fooled me and lived instead
It grew to be my mother's pride and joy

It's just an old magnolia tree
But friend it means much more to me
It's the symbol of my mother's tender love
And of all the things in life I've found
That picked me up when I was down
I remember my magnolia mother's love

The kinfolk come and stood around
The day we laid my momma down
I swore I'd try to be a better man
Standing there beneath her favorite tree
I knew her pride and joy was me
When a petal fell and nestled in my hand

It's just an old magnolia tree
But friend it means much more to me
It's the symbol of my mother's tender love
And of all the things in life I've found
That picked me up when I was down
I remember my magnolia mother's love

MERRY CHRISTMAS TO YOU

BY BILLY JOE SHAVER
(BMI)

Merry Christmas to you, Merry Christmas to you
Merry Christmas, Merry Christmas to you
May your prayers and your dreams of a lifetime come true
Merry Christmas, Merry Christmas to you

God's only son on this same day was born
Merry Christmas, Merry Christmas to you
And for those who believe, He's the gift we receive
Merry Christmas, Merry Christmas to you

Merry Christmas to you, Merry Christmas to you
Merry Christmas, Merry Christmas to you
Merry Christmas to you, Merry Christmas to you
Merry Christmas, Merry Christmas to you

On that wonderful day, Christ Jesus will say
Merry Christmas, Merry Christmas to you
When he comes with his angels to save us away
Merry Christmas, Merry Christmas to you

All the church bells will ring, all God's children will sing
Merry Christmas, Merry Christmas to you
When together we fly to our home in the sky
Merry Christmas, Merry Christmas to you

Printed in the USA
CPSIA information can be obtained
at www.ICGtesting.com
LVHW091919110224
771149LV00005BA/22